Craig Borlase

purepop?

the Delirious? journey so far

Furious?
Records   **Published by Furious? Records**

Published by Furious? Records
PO Box 3038
Littlehampton
West Sussex
BN17 5SZ

First Published in Great Britain 1998
British Library Cataloguing-in-Publication Data
A CIP catalogue for this book can be obtained from the British Library.
ISBN 0 9534647 0 9

Designed by Furious? Records
Printed and bound in Great Britain by Halcyon, Heathfield, East Sussex

All photography by Andy Hutch except page 53, by Ben Cloney

Special thanks to all at Furious? Records, especially Nykki, Giles, Tony and Emma. To Jill Stevens, Mike P, Mrs Borlase, Andy Hutch, the Delirious? ladies and, of course, the boys themselves.

Contents

Foreword:

If you could have been with me five years ago, you would have met my friends, Stu G the electrician, Jon the art student, Stew the graphic designer and Tim the studio owner. We were a very extra normal bunch of guys, just doing what everyone else does; working hard, earning a living and dreaming big dreams. The veneer of Delirious? has changed somewhat in that time, but deep at the core you can still find the same old characters: backstage before a gig or round the meal table, amazed at God's grace and incredible sense of humour. In many ways it still feels like the beginning of the journey, and we hope this book will give you a small insight into our lives over the last few years. As ever, thank you for your support. I believe the best is yet to come.

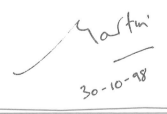

Martin
30-10-98

Preface

I was sitting at the back of an increasingly sweaty Leeds Town & Country Club, doing a good job of soaking up the vibes given out by five young men who like to finish their band name with a question mark. I counted myself a lucky man but I'm not altogether sure why. I reckoned that I could have been seeing the start of something big, but then again tape-buyers, concert-goers and all sorts of d:junkies had been feeling like that since the band first stumbled, half-formed, into the public half-light five years before. The then-named Cutting Edge Band did things on the worship scene, and the band that I was watching were tickling the mainstream with their blend of upwardly-focused chunky sounds. In their first year of working their mojo in the UK charts the boys notched up two top 20 singles, a top 13 album and... well, all sorts of other things. But in the jigsaw conversations we all had at the time, the curious thing seemed to be that, although they were certainly pleased with the story so far, it was very much a 'so far' kind of story. When they chanted the tune-led lyrics 'I want to go deeper', you knew they meant it, despite the fact no one was exactly sure where Deeper was.

And today, nearly two years on, people are still unsure. People ask the band if they're going to be like X, or whether they're going to follow in the footsteps of Y. The answer is always a gentle shrug and a vague 'perhaps'. Nobody knows what's going to happen because nobody's really done it before.

Remembering that time in Leeds again there is one incident that sticks out, bolder than the rest. On a visit to a local radio station the DJ started to chat:

'When we got 'Deeper',' he said, 'we put it on thinking we were going to get yet another '90s guitar band. But after the first few bars something kind of shone about it that lifted it above the rest. Is that something you do consciously?'

We laughed.

While writing this I have built up a big debt to many people: most of them at Furious? Records. In all the time that I've known Delirious? - some of it when I've worked for them, some of it when I haven't - the five 'boys' have always talked a fair bit about the future. This book comes out at a time when much of that chat could well become reality. If there's one thing this book does for you, hopefully it will let you know that their aims and attitudes will remain the same.

Craig Borlase, 1998

part 1: *poppeople*

Public address

Introduction

The story of Delirious? rambles across a handful of decades. Throughout it all, the pace varies. At times the story pauses, seeking direction, its key players wondering where things should go. There are other times, too, when everything steams ahead, full of purpose, seemingly unstoppable. This is the way it has always been: progress coming when it will, destination unknown.

Made up of males, Delirious? is no boy-band, their birth planned from the leathered marketing suite of a major label. In part they are here by accident (yes, the sort involving cars).

Delirious? shouldn't be successful. By all rights their success is wrong. First up are the people: an age gap lies within the band, wide enough to swallow a whole generation. Together, Stu G and Jon form the bread in a 'time sandwich', the fillings including Finger Pop, Mop Tops, Flower Power, Motown, Psychedelic Rock, Folk Rock, Glam Rock, Disco and Punk. Theory might suggest that the guitarist is old enough (biologically, although not legally) to be the bassist's father. Yet they are friends. The other three, while balancing out the age-old see-saw, present the collective with even more differences when it comes to their trades: a businessman, a record producer and a graphic designer. Their lack of common ground could lead to a conclusion that working together is difficult, their histories and skills setting them apart.

But if you're looking for differences, for reasons why this d:thing should never have made it out of the nursery, the search is over once you get to the music. The five of them combine to make a musical history so diverse that it sounds like the plot for some particularly bad musical. Hidden beneath the solid beats and anthemic choruses are musical educations received at some frighteningly different schools: Heavy Rock, Funk, Alternative, AOR, Children's Entertainment. Those who have never heard the sound of Delirious? would be forgiven for being worried about it.

Surely with these backgrounds, they would conclude, the baby Delirious? should never have made it? Shouldn't someone have done the decent thing and kept it quiet?

What started with a pic 'n' mix of musical ambition has now become a united force. What started as five strangers separated by miles and years has grown into a family. This is the story of how it happened.

What started **as five** strangers separated by miles and **years** has grown into a family

This is the **story of** how it

happened

Tim

Tim Jupp was born in the first week of 1966, a few months before England's World Cup victory, and a few years before the explosion of Culture from which Delirious? would come. Not that he knew much of this, for his early childhood was spent in Eastbourne. People have always retired to Eastbourne, and a birth there is big news.

Tim's father, Ebby, worked for a chain of estate agents, and stepped in as manager whenever new branches were set up. This meant the whole family - Tim, his parents and his older sister, Nykki, and younger brother, Andy - had to move area whenever necessary. The first move came for Tim when he was five years old. The family left the purple-rinse of Eastbourne for Bexhill-on-Sea, another 'nice' town on the South Coast.

It was at this age that Tim's parents encouraged their eldest son to take up the piano. Signs of musical genius were slow to emerge, but Tim passed his Grade I exam within three years. However, instead of practising, he spent much of this time complaining to his parents about how much he hated the instrument. It took another couple of years before they gave in, but not without so rightly pointing out that one day, Tim would 'be grateful that he had those lessons'.

The act of giving up did not signify the start of a character rebellion. Tim quickly filled the time-hole created by the absence of piano tuition with musical study of a different kind: this time playing the trumpet. Progress then was much more immediate, and within two years he passed his Grade VI exam with top marks.

At the age of 12 it was easy to see those parts of Tim's character that would go on to be dominant in his adult life. A total enthusiast, Tim found something about the trumpet 'that just clicked'. Where he had struggled to find the motivation to pursue the piano, his natural talent as a horn player gave him enough of a kick-start to practise to an almost obsessive degree.

This 'all or nothing' approach also served him well in other areas of life. As he moved into his teens he developed a certain talent as an athlete. A few good results on the track were enough of an encouragement to get him out fitness training every day. Before going to school Tim would train for half an hour, working on his 100 and 200 metre sprints. By the age of 15 he was in the top ten for his age group across the county.

As with the trumpet, Tim was supported and encouraged by his parents, but the primary motivation, the force which led him to be quite so dedicated, came from within. If he didn't like it, he wouldn't do it. On the other hand, once he found something that got him going, Tim would pursue it with every bit of energy he had.

When he was 13 it was time for the family to move again; this time to Worthing, where Ebby Jupp was to set up another local branch. This was a difficult time for Tim: he had settled in well at his previous secondary school and was finding friendships through his various activities. Worthing meant not only a new school, but a new athletics club, music teacher and church. Overnight, almost everything in his life changed.

Tim arrived at Durrington High School, Worthing, in 1979, at the start of his Fourth Year. 'It was very difficult to make friends; everyone was already part of a group. For the first year I struggled to break in.'

Perhaps in a subconscious way Tim was trying to return to Bexhill-on-Sea, for every Saturday he cycled 15 miles in the direction of his old home town to watch Brighton Hove Albion play football.

The Jupp family had always been regular church-goers. Like many children, Tim had gone along quite happily, but only felt a sense of personal faith when he got a little older.

'Each Sunday,' says Tim 'either my mother or father would go to church in the evening, leaving the other one to look after us children. We were never allowed to watch TV on Sundays, so we often used to get around the piano and sing a few songs. I remember once singing a song that said Happy Birthday to Jesus. I turned to my mum and said, "I wish I could have another birthday." She told me that I could, so we had a little chat, said a prayer, and that was it. I had become a Christian.'

When the family moved to Worthing they all started going to a new church. One reason in particular that got Tim excited about going was Ron, an ex semi-professional jazz pianist: 'He used to play this Steinway grand piano in a way that had me amazed.' Before long, Tim was back to his first instrument, this time determined to do well.

A music student told him how to work out chords - advice which set him off playing at home. Now he could easily play the songs that he had been singing at church. Tim soon received another boost from church when he was asked to join the team that played during special monthly meetings. These meetings grew in size until there were as many as 1200 people attending. By the time he was 16, Tim was in charge of the band, a responsibility that made him very happy.

Things at school, however, were not going quite so well. Although he had passed his O Levels, he found the atmosphere uninviting. Instead of staying on for the Sixth Form, Tim decided to carry on with his A Levels at the local college. This gave him time to pursue a new interest. While playing keyboards with another band, he had made friends with the person who took care of the PA. Tim began to help him as he set up a business, going out with him to carry the gear and help set it up. The technical side of this work appealed, particularly as he was studying for his Maths A Level.

The routine of working with his friend for as many as three nights per week, as well as throughout the weekend, took its toll on Tim's studies. He would get home late at night from a job and miss the next day's lectures in favour of learning his choruses for the following Sunday. The exams came and went and Tim failed them all. His parents were disappointed, although they had learnt by now that their son would do well, but only if he enjoyed what he was doing.

As a musician Tim was becoming increasingly in demand. A couple of years previously, a man named Ishmael had heard his playing at one of the church meetings and invited him to join his band for a week-long gig at a festival. It had gone well, and Tim was now a regular member of the band that was having a big impact on the Christian children's music scene in the country.

The band appealed to a part of Tim's character that had perhaps been hidden at school. At times he could be naturally exuberant and flamboyant - qualities that made him ideal for the band. Since moving, he had never truly settled at school, and had always been on the fringes of the groups formed before he arrived. With music, things were different: he was confident in his abilities and one hundred per cent committed. Without knowing how, he and others began to wonder whether it might be possible for him to make a career out of it.

Those decisions were a long way off, though, and at the age of 18 Tim was in need of a job that paid there and then. He eventually found one at National Westminster Bank in Storrington, just ten miles from home. The nine-to-five structure suited him: it meant that he didn't have to change his commitments to the various musical enterprises that carried his mark at the time.

Work carried on in this way for a couple of years, 'until my boss ruined it all' says Tim. 'One day he called me into his office and asked me the question that finished my career there: "Do you see yourself doing my job when you're my age?".' In response Tim had little option but to tell the truth. 'I liked him, and I couldn't lie to him. So I told him, "no, I won't be here when I'm your age." After that they gave up on me, and used me as a spare part, a relief cashier, who filled in for people when they were sick. I decided to hand my notice in soon after that. I told

Ishmael that I was going to go full-time with him. He couldn't pay me, but I was just so keen to be involved with music.'

To help finance this venture, Tim became a qualified bus driver, and worked with a small firm who took people to school and work. This meant getting up at five, but it also meant that much of the day was his own. By 9.30am he would be out with his friend cleaning windows, earning a couple of pounds per hour. By 2.30pm Tim would be heading back to the bus to take people home. The weekends were spent travelling to gigs with Ishmael. Life was hectic and Tim loved it.

By the time he was 20 Tim was beginning to get paid by Ishmael. Instead of travelling, the band were working in the studio, producing tapes that were selling well. Their studio of choice was ICC (International Christian Communication) in Eastbourne. It was there, in 1987, that Tim met Martin Smith, aged 17.

Despite his early impression of Martin as 'basically the tea boy... very quiet and shy', the two of them became friends over the years, as Tim and the band spent more time in the studio. When Tim married Becca Thatcher in 1990, he invited Martin to the wedding. It was there that Martin met Becca's younger sister Anna, who he would later marry.

Tim's business brain soon began to function, however, when he thought about the amount of time and money they were spending in the studio. He worked out that it might be cheaper to start buying his own gear. And so Tim's first proper career began. He bought a computer and started to program the band's next batch of material. With the money set aside for the next tape, he bought a 16-track recording machine and recorded the tracks in his old bedroom at his parents' house.

Soon Martin and Tim had become close friends, sharing an interest not only in music production, but in the whole area of worship and music in church.

'We only lived an hour away from Martin at this point, and whenever he had a break, he would come over and hang out. I can remember Martin arriving at all times of the day and night - usually once he had finished a session and had the next day off. Along with Becca we used to spend hours talking about worship.'

Often Martin would tell them about a man he had met in America called Kevin Prosch. Through his work, many people were discovering new things about music: about its power, about its potential.

Also included in these discussions was Stewart Smith - freshly introduced to God and the church. They naturally formed a friendship, not only because of their musical connections, but because of a shared passion for getting something going for the young people both in and outside of the church.

Throughout the time spent talking with one another there was an undercurrent of excitement: not because of a glimpsed future, but stemming simply from a belief that something could be done - about people and music - and that perhaps they could be part of the plan.

This 'all or nothing' approach also served him well in other areas of life

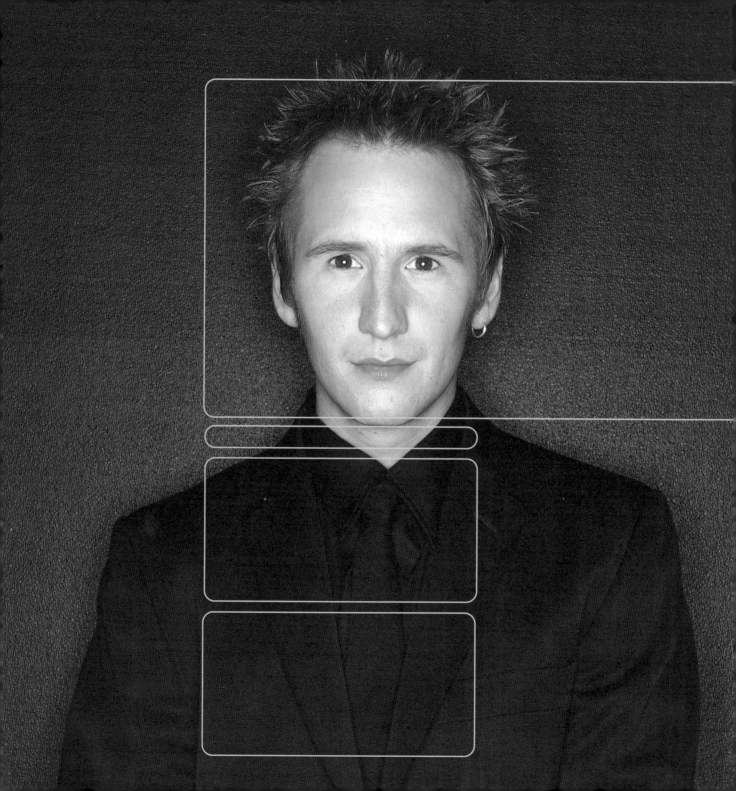

Martin

Like Tim, Martin also spent much of his early life caught between two worlds. At home there was the security of strong beliefs, while at school he felt overwhelmed by a sense of non-belonging. Of all the relationships between the Delirious? members today, the bond between Martin and Tim is perhaps the strongest. Between them is the longest friendship and the shared interests of sound recording. On a deeper level, their school experiences are similar. At times both found school a difficult place to be; both made decisions soon after leaving school to build their careers around the Christian music scene.

Martin was born in Woodford Green, Essex, in 1970. He got off to a fairly shaky start in that, although his birth went smoothly enough, Martin contracted bronchial pneumonia and was placed in an iron lung - a device designed to keep him breathing. His parents anxiously waited for some noise to come from him, for a sign that his lungs were working properly. 'God,' they prayed, 'if you can give our son a voice, then he'll be yours.' After two weeks he cried, and his life began again.

Edwin and Sylvia Smith had four children: Paul and Pete, the elder brothers, Martin and his younger sister, Suzi. The Smiths all attended their local Brethren Church - a branch where structure, order and respect were high on the list of maintenance priorities. Hats played a part too: the women were encouraged to keep theirs on.

'My life became very organised,' says Martin. 'My dad had a nine-to-five job, so things were pretty much the same every day.' Sunday was no exception to this, and helped to provide Martin with a deep-rooted sense of security: church in the morning, a guest for Sunday lunch, church in the evening.

'I had a very happy childhood, even though, looking back, Church often felt quite religious...' But for Martin the meal table was a place where 'religion' would be discussed; where issues could be explained. And so Christianity and all the business that goes with it was woven into the everyday fabric of Martin's life. Beliefs were never something to be embarrassed about, and nor were they something to be kept solely for special occasions. As an adult Martin has kept hold of this, and although the band don't have a power hierarchy, it is often Martin who will take the lead in steering gigs into spontaneous, overtly God-focused sections.

One thing there was less of in the Smith family home was music. Of all the members in the band, Martin's musical education is the most bizarre. Apart from Abba (courtesy of his eldest brother), there was little music played in the house.

'None of my family were really into music at all. The only records my dad played were middle-of-the-road Christian gospel records - all choirs and hymnals.' The trait passed from father to son, and it was only in his late teens that Martin started buying albums. His first attempt at this was a failure, however. At the height of U2's first wave of success, *The Joshua Tree* hit the shops. Having bought his own copy and given it a dutiful listening to, Martin took it back to the shop because he didn't think it was up to much. Few would argue with his suggestion that in those days he 'had a lot to learn'.

Strangely, Martin can remember having piano lessons at the age of eight. The reason for their starting is as unclear as the reason for their ending after only a few months. Four years later Martin got hold of his first guitar - bought by his dad - and taught himself how to play. Like Tim, the church became a focus for his musical enthusiasm, and the congregation was regularly treated to songs performed by Martin at various meetings and services. To his surprise now, Martin's first gigs were delivered to the public through an old keyboard amp, a tired microphone and a poor quality spring reverb unit.

Even though Martin grew up in a less 'musical' household than some of his co-members, he didn't waste time getting down to business. 'It just seemed totally natural to me: I had a guitar, so I wrote songs.' Early subject matter was linked by a couple of themes - girls and faith.

Martin's age put him in the last group to suffer the Eleven plus examination system. Pupils' choices of secondary schools depended on their results in the exam. Martin managed to scrape enough marks to secure a place at the prestigious local grammar school. It was there that Martin encountered his first challenges to his beliefs. It was an all-male school, where academic progress was valued above everything else. For those like Martin who weren't in the top half, it could seem like the whole system was against you.

School life was made more difficult by Martin's beliefs. 'I was the one Christian kid in the class, and had been brought up to stand my ground whenever it came to a question of faith.' This led to 'an incredible tension' in the classroom. He knew that he was different, yet he wanted to be like his classmates. 'At times it was strange; I had the words and all the right things to say, but deep down I just didn't always have the character to back them up.'

The one area that did offer him a chance to join in and be part of things was sport. Where the family home had been missing music, it had sport up to its roof. From an early age, all the children were encouraged to play as much as possible. Once at school, Martin showed a natural ability at a wide range of sports. He captained the cricket, hockey and soccer teams, but this was still not enough to provide him with a sense of belonging alongside his peers.

The influence of the church on Martin was so strong that it affected everything he did. Aged 15 he was offered the chance to play for the county schools' cricket team. As most of the team's matches were played on a Sunday morning, there was no way he was going to be able to accept. The decision was not made for him - although there obviously was influence from his parents - it mainly came from Martin's sense of what he thought was right.

'I can remember desperately wanting to be a part of the team, but knowing that regularly missing church for a sports match felt wrong at that time. I constantly lived with that tension: on the one hand knowing that there were plenty of people who were doing it (Christians included), but on the other knowing that this was the way I wanted to live. Even as a small child I knew that.'

At one particularly wild school disco, the class's number one bully was getting out of his face on Shandy Bass. He was sick, and Martin decided to help out by taking him home. On the way he was treated to a drunken speech in his praise: '*Martian....Martian...your ver best bloak. Know one else would of done this. I luv ewe....*'

Back in school on Monday and the Shandy fan was back, arms raised in triumph, ready to get back to the job of giving young Smith a good verbal kicking.

Academically, Martin remained in the bottom half of the class. Whereas his friends were passing ten O Levels each, Martin only managed to pass two (English Literature and Pottery). Because of these results he had to repeat the year. Instead of crushing him, it turned out to be the best year he spent at school. Given a fresh start, he managed to make a new set of friends.

There was one other event that made the year go with a swing. Martin had entered the BBC Song for Christmas competition, and unexpectedly won second prize. This meant a trip to Birmingham to perform the song on national prime-time television. The next day at school he had been transformed from an academic write-off to a musical hero, giving a special performance in front of the whole school.

The song had come out of playing around at home with a four-track recorder. Now Martin began to take music more seriously, thinking of ways in which he could fulfil his ultimate ambition of being a 'pop star'. Staying on at school for A Levels was out of the question, so he applied for a YTS (Youth Training Scheme).

In the Easter holidays of his final year at school, Martin spent one week working as a tape copier at the big Christian festival, Spring Harvest. This meant recording seminars, but more importantly, gave him the chance to get to know people from ICC - the largest Christian-run studios in the country. Persuading them to take him on as part of his YTS wasn't too difficult: he had shown some talent and they wouldn't have to pay him.

The following August, with four O Levels to his name, Martin moved to Eastbourne to start work. What followed was a tidal wave of musical education.

'For a whole year I immersed myself in everything to do with music. I stayed up all hours learning how to use microphones and mixing desks and sitting in on sessions. We would have anything from Christian bands to Opera singers to Heavy Metal bands come in and use the studio. I found something good in every bit of music that I heard. My world was beginning to open.'

For the boy who had found one of the previous decade's biggest selling albums 'a bit boring', ICC had a lot to teach him. Within weeks his mind had been opened and he began to see music for what it was. Within six months Martin was recording sessions in his own right, specialising in live bands and live albums.

Listening to the pile-up of musical styles taught him one lesson that would be more valuable to him than any other: to recognise the sound of a great song.

'I would be listening and constantly asking myself why one song sounded better than another, what made things work. Looking back, I was getting trained to be a songwriter.'

When he was 19 Martin was sent to record the live album at a new Christian conference called New Wine. Meeting the band there was his first encounter with people from the Vineyard branch of churches - an American-based movement that was pioneering a low-key, yet profoundly intimate, style of worshipping God. As he listened to the music something happened. He returned home different: God had touched him, and his view of Christianity shifted from being cerebral to being one of an intimate friendship with God. The next day he wrote the song 'Lord You Have My Heart' - one which clearly maps out his new-style relationship with God.

In an uncharacteristic burst of recklessness, Martin immediately went back to his boss to see if he could take all his holiday in one chunk. A couple of months later he was on his way to Vancouver and LA to stay with some of the musicians he had met at the conference.

'At the time it was a bit lonely and I wondered what I was really there for. Once I got to LA I bumped into this poodle-haired southerner called Kevin Prosch. I didn't know it at the time, but he was another musician from the church. What I did know instantly was that we had hit it off.'

At a service a couple of days later, Martin was surprised to see Kevin up on stage, leading the worship. The way he played and led the band and the congregation, as well as the songs he had written, left Martin speechless. This was something brand new, something to be savoured.

'He was cheeky, free to be himself and loved the music. I knew that I was watching something that I identified with.'

Over the next week the two spent time together, Kevin giving him a pre-mix tape of his new album, *Even So, Come*. On the way home Martin listened to it non-stop, in tears. The three-week holiday had become a pilgrimage, and he was bringing something back.

Martin returned to Eastbourne and started a band. Musically, Hope Train was about as different to Delirious? as you can imagine: a funky outfit with neat guitars and a low-key stage show. However, their purpose marked them out as an early test-run for Delirious?. Martin was fired up about taking spiritual music - worship music - out into the mainstream. Hope Train offered him his first journeys out

of the Christian scene and into the pubs and clubs of Eastbourne.

It was also at this time that Martin had another experience that he would draw on in later life. While working at ICC, the studios were booked by Radio One for three days of interviews with Paul McCartney. They were recording a series called 'McCartney on McCartney' - quite simply a very long chat with the man about anything and everything. Martin was Tape-Op and got to listen to everything, changing the reels of tape every time they ran out. Apart from the fact that he was Paul McCartney, the thing that impressed Martin was that he had chosen to record at ICC, not because it was the best studio, but because it was the one closest to his home and family. At the end of each day Paul would be back at home, making sure his priorities were in order.

One of the first people that Martin was keen to talk to when he returned from America was Tim. They had been meeting each other over the previous few months, and Martin had immediately liked this 'bouncy, smiley chap.'

After the trip, the time Tim and Martin spent together was focused on where Christian music was heading.

'We talked about it loads and tried to get to grips with it. I'd been exposed to every sort of music that was coming out of the church, and I often wondered why it didn't sound as good as the stuff I was buying in the high street. Obviously the financial restrictions of recording for a smaller market had an impact, but at times some of the material seemed to lack passion and emotion.'

Together they wondered why the music seemed to be less concerned with performance or artistry, in favour of producing something quick and cheap. Soon Martin had moved over to Rustington to be part of Tim's church - Arun Community Church. Having visited it months earlier, Martin was sure that it was the right place for him to be. Within days he was going out with Anna Thatcher, the pastor's youngest daughter, and planning with Tim and

Becca how they could make good music and get it out to the people.

Alongside his experiences in California, Martin was beginning to sense the outlines of a plot, getting increasingly excited about what lay ahead. Many were inspired by the songs they were hearing on the UK Christian scene, but the affect on Martin was particularly strong. This was a good time to be interested in Christianity and music. Martin met and became friends with the likes of Graham Kendrick, Noel Richards and Matt Redman, all through being asked to engineer or produce their albums. He also became good friends with Les Moir, producer and A&R man for Christian label, Kingsway. Les often used Martin to engineer, and spent countless hours working with him on various projects.

'I remember working on one of Noel's albums (*Thunder In The Skies*), and finishing regularly at four or five in the morning while we were mixing it. Les was a complete perfectionist and would drive me crazy at the time. Looking back, though, his incredible attention to detail rubbed off on me and has stuck with me while working on the Delirious? projects.

It just seemed **totally natural** to me: I had a **guitar**, so I **wrote songs**

The three-week holiday had become a pilgrimage, and he was bringing something back

Stew

Stewart Smith throws in a handful of contradictions to the story. Although his musical background is more acceptable for a muso (far more than Tim's children's work or Martin's musical drought), he admits that he never wanted to be a musician. Even when the band had been together for years, it remained a hobby for the drummer.

Stewart Smith - later christened Stew Schmee by the band - was born in 1968. Having a brother just five minutes younger meant that childhood was going to be marked by either companionship or competition. Luckily, the competition remained at the easy level of friendly rivalry, and Nigel and Stew shared a happy childhood.

Sport played a big part in their lives. 'Being a twin meant that I always had someone to play with,' says Stew. Favoured activities included tennis, football and snooker - one-on-one games that tested physical and mental powers.

The location of the Smith family - the parents and their two boys - changed only a couple of times. When the boys were born they lived in Lingford, moving later to East Preston: both towns around the Littlehampton area. When they were ten years old they moved to Bognor Regis, a few miles down the coast. For many people in England, Bognor Regis is a name that brings a smile to the face, its ugly name pushing it to the top of the 'Easy Places To Joke About' lists.

At home Stew had become a keen Drummer's Anorak. The Thursday-night ritual of watching 'Top of the Pops' always guaranteed a good five or six drummers for Stew to watch and then demonstrate his skill as an air-drummer. The reason for the interest in drums is unclear: 'I don't know why, but I always liked the drums.' An early favourite was Rick Butler from The Jam. Years later Stew would meet his early hero and his influence would have a lasting effect on Stew. For now he was content to watch him on TV.

When he was 14, Stew's grandfather died, leaving him £100. Having decided that it was a drum kit that he wanted, Stew found one for sale in the local paper and bought it. 'Once I got it home I realised that I didn't even know how to set it up.' Instead of having lessons, Stew taught himself by playing along to albums on his stereo. 'It was just fun. No one ever told me to practise, so it was just my thing. When I got home from school I always used to mess about on it for a couple of hours.'

With a couple of years of after-school drumming under his belt, Stew moved up to the next level and answered an advert for a drummer he had seen in a local music shop. The band was called Manner of Mind, and the guy who was advertising was in his late twenties. The rest of the band were a little younger, but at 16, Stew was easily the youngest member.

The band played at various pubs in the area. Little Stew would have to get a lift there from his dad, who would dutifully sit through three hours of Folk-Rock before taking his son home.

'We used to play for £30, which would get split between the whole band. If we were lucky, they might throw in a few sandwiches too. My family were great about it. I was moving away from sport, but my brother was doing well and playing for the county. They managed to make us both feel like what we were doing was important.'

At this level - playing the odd gig when it came up - Stew was happy. Being in a band was something that he had wanted to do since those early days spent watching 'Top of the Pops'. Unlike many others, Stew didn't feel the desire to be playing full-time. He wanted to earn some money. This meant leaving school and pursuing an interest in art by working at a local graphic design agency. The low pay for low jobs situation passed after a couple of months when he was taken on full-time and given training as a designer. Once he was 17 Stew bought a car, and before

long this Soul Boy was a familiar sight around Bognor. His flick-style haircut, waffle jumpers and gold jewellery made him identifiable; his Chrysler Alpine with '*If it moves, funk it*' sun visa made him unforgettable.

Stew's opinion of church had never risen very high. As a child, the family had made a handful of visits, but Stew had been bored each time. To him it was 'dull and irrelevant', and he didn't expect to have anything more to do with it. His opinions softened a little once he discovered Soul and Gospel music. An old friend from school had got into church having gone on a drugs bender the year before. He told Stew about a Gospel band that he wanted to start, and along with other friends from their schooldays, Stew got involved.

'I was just interested in the music, really,' he says. 'I wasn't that bothered about the beliefs, although I did start asking a few questions.'

It was partly through his first job that Stew became a Christian. He met a man named Andy Milne who worked at the same company. The two became friends and Stew was quickly impressed by Andy's personality.

'He seemed to know exactly where he was going in life, as if he understood things that I had never thought about. He was a great guy with an excellent sense of humour, and it was the silly things that made me take his religion seriously.'

Stew fired questions at him over the next two years: from sex to death to suffering. Without any flashes of light or visits from angels, Stew began to believe. The moment he went along to Andy's church was the moment that he knew he was a Christian.

When he was 21 the design agency was bought out, but within six months it had gone bankrupt. Stew was rewarded for his years of work with a redundancy package. He left the office, bought a new drum kit, took a week-long holiday, and walked into another job as a

freelance designer. 'I earned more money in a week than I used to earn in a month. I couldn't believe my luck.'

The job only lasted a week, though, as Stew was bored. Instead, he took his portfolio around to various companies, and after a few days landed a job at Designline, on the outskirts of Portsmouth. For three years he stayed there, gaining more experience and improving his design skills.

In his spare time Stew was teaching drums at a local girls' school, and one of his pupils got round to telling him about her church, inviting him along. The first time Stew went to Arun Community Church he loved it, and has stayed there ever since.

'Beofre I visited Arun I had gone along to Andy's church, and I didn't know that there was any other style. It wasn't until later that I found out that were other alternatives. Having a full band playing at the front of church was a big deal.

'I met Tim on my first visit. I was a bit shy, only knowing one person there, but Tim came up and was really friendly right from the start.'

Tim had been at the church for a while, and had been playing during the services. Another musician was a good find for a Sunday morning, especially a drummer. After a few weeks Stew was playing alongside Tim at church.

But church also gave Stew something else to get excited about. Having met and liked Sarah Thatcher (another daughter of the pastor), he started to get involved, with her and a few others, in the church's youth work.

'Before long you begin to see patterns in people's lives: you see people come and go. Some are inspired to make a difference, others just drift along. Every couple of years the whole youth group seems to leave and go to college; it feels like you're starting again.'

This realisation that time was precious got the team

thinking about how they could best use it. Together they desperately wanted to do something that would make a lasting difference to the people they met.

It is clear to see how what Stew does today relates to his past: his eye for good visuals and image clearly comes from his work as a designer. On another level, we can see the signs that were pointing towards the Stew Smith that is so easy to get along with today: his knack for making people feel comfortable was obviously at work when he joined the band that was made up of people much older than him. The side of Stew that wants to see people looked after, that wants the band to be a loud voice in pop culture, is strongly linked to the fact that he grew up with no real knowledge of God.

His flick-style haircut waffle jumpers and gold jewellery made him identifiable; his Chrysler Alpine with

'If it moves, funk it'

sun visa made him unforgettable

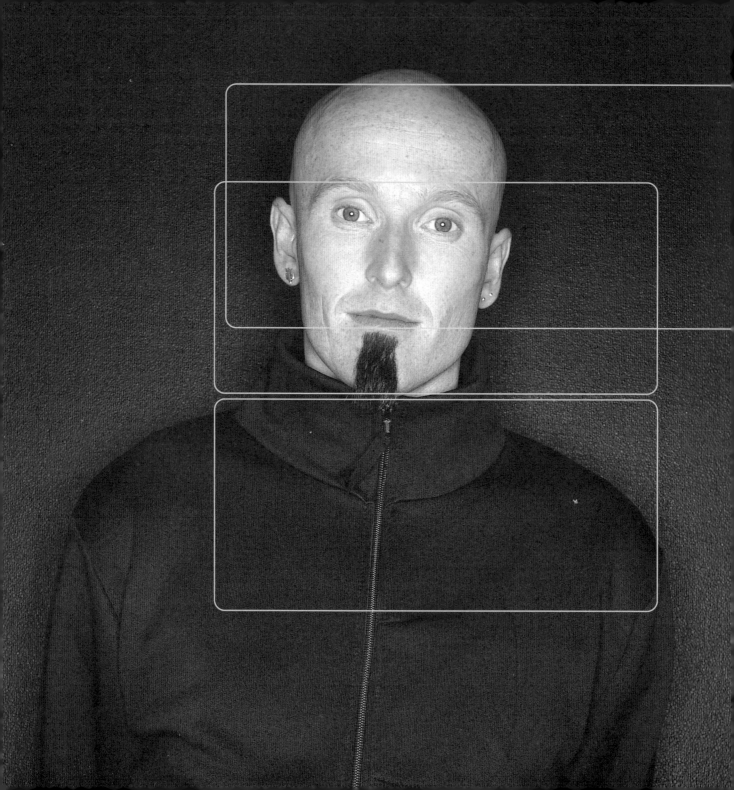

Stu G

For Stuart David Garrard, change has been something he has welcomed throughout his life. New experiences find him at the head of the queue, eager to taste something fresh, to find out more. From a childhood spent in Ipswich to an early adult life in London, Stu G has learnt the lessons of his life from a variety of textbooks.

Dave and Viv Garrard have three children: a daughter either side of their only son - Debbie being the eldest and Pippa the youngest. Stu was born in 1963, and stayed around the Ipswich area almost constantly until he was 23.

'I only have happy memories of my childhood,' says Stu. 'Like visiting the hardware store that my granddad owned and buying sixpence-worth of 'stales' from the bakery next door. I'd end up with this massive bag of cakes that were about to go off, trying to eat as many as possible.'

Family holidays in Cornwall, life sandwiched between two sisters, and trips to the barbers all went into the mix as well. Stu went through Sunday School from the age of five, and then graduated to Boys' Brigade. The latter provided him with all the things that boys like (especially when they're in a Brigade): endless games of football and camping trips away where the art of survival could be mastered. The one slight cloud on the horizon was school: Stu found himself in a rut of being 'the slow one' when it came to sport. He was also was carrying a substantial amount of cement around in his mouth (braces) and had his fair share of nicknames. When he was 14 his parents (who managed sheltered accommodation for the elderly) had to move 12 miles away to Felixstowe, and the whole family went with them.

'Starting a new school was nerve-racking, but it did me loads of good in terms of confidence.' The fresh start was enough to get Stu playing football and making the school team. When the family moved back to Ipswich 15 months later, Stu spent a final year at his old school 'that was fantastic; an average nobody had left the school, and on return I was good at a couple of things.'

Long before shuttling between schools, Stu G had been getting seriously into music, thanks to a record collection that his uncle had left round at his granddad's. Whenever he could, Stu would listen to 'She Loves You', 'I Want To Hold Your Hand' or '1,2,3' (the collection was small). He took to miming along to the music, although it wasn't the guitar lines he was picking out, but the drumming.

'I had this little wooden desk that I used to pretend was a drum kit. Sometimes I'd get my mum's pots and pans out and hit them instead.'

Like Stew, Stu G was an avid 'Top Of The Pops' watcher, although the age gap meant that his viewing caught the Jimmy Saville/black-and-white era. Regular appearances were made by such legends as The Beatles and The Rolling Stones.

The early enthusiasm for drumming continued, and when he was 14, Stu's parents sent him off to have lessons. He soon bought a kit and spent the following couple of years playing in his bedroom. Something changed when he was 16 that was to affect the rest of his life.

'It was the first time that I had ever heard any of Queen's stuff; they had a single out called 'Killer Queen'. Something about their sound and attitude really inspired me. From that moment on I knew I wanted to be Brian May.'

The drum kit got sold and an electric guitar was bought in its place. Stu was following the Rock theme, and consequently discovered other bands like Boston and Rush. Trying to emulate the heavily distorted sound proved to be a slight problem for the young axe-man: his amplifier could only manage a five-Watt whisper. Not to be deterred, Stu found a way around the problem:

'If I turned it up to full volume, placed it face down on the bed and covered it with a sleeping bag I had myself a wicked distortion sound.'

For a whole year he spent most of his spare time learning Queen songs in his room. After that he left the house for lessons with a private tutor. It wasn't until Stu reached 18 that he started to play in public.

'The first thing I did was a musical at church. Although I'd been brought up to go to church, I'd never really enjoyed it or been remotely interested in what it was about, but some friends were into it and they needed a guitarist for the band.'

After the musical the band stayed together, naming themselves 33 Across.

When he was 16 Stu had left school to take up an apprenticeship with the electricity board. His dad was a carpenter, and he encouraged his son to get a trade for himself. Having had a friend who had gone down the same route a couple of years before, Stu thought being an electrician would be his best bet. For the first year of his apprenticeship he moved to Romford, Essex, to the company's training centre.

Once he was there he began to miss friends from home, as well the chance to play guitar - his bulky equipment was not easily transported. However, Stu found the experience to be character forming, choosing to get on with the job of learning what was needed.

'A lot of the instructors were from another era: they seemed more like drill sergeants than lecturers. Something of that discipline has stayed with me though. And at the time I knew it was a good experience for me.'

Although he didn't get much time to play, he had plenty of time to watch. Whenever it was possible, Stu would go off to the Ilford Palais or the Hammersmith Odeon to see whatever band was playing. Favourites were always the likes of Ian Dury and the Blockheads, Elvis Costello and the

Attractions, or XTC: bands with an extra dimension to their music.

One type of music that Stu went out of his way to avoid was the Christian sort. Childhood experiences of church had made him wonder why, if Christianity was so good, did everyone look so miserable? The whole thing seemed to Stu to be a pale reflection of life. Christian music was the same - trying to imitate the pop scene, but failing miserably.

This attitude went out of the window as soon as he heard Phil Keaggy, an American guitarist well known for his skilful technique and Christian beliefs. Stu had moved back to Ipswich after his year of training, and had heard a recording while at his elder sister's house. He was immediately hooked, and knew that he had to see Phil Keaggy live.

Together with his fiancee, Karen, he planned a trip to London to see Keaggy's next gig and to stay with a couple of friends in town. Ken and Von Humphries happened to be Christians, and the combination of a great gig followed by a gospel message from the stage, as well as a couple of days talking it over with their friends, meant that Stu and Karen returned home to Ipswich as Christians.

There then followed a hectic period. Stu started writing songs and playing them to friends the couple were meeting on their regular trips to London. They married in 1984 and soon gave up their jobs (a career in banking for Karen) and their home town, and left for London. Ken and Von (who also happened to be related to the Garrards) had invited them to come and stay with them, to join in with Ken's job. Stu was to travel with him as he preached, starting the meetings with a few songs. Since neither of them had spent much time in church before then, Stu and Karen were learning lots each day.

'After a couple of years of that we all moved to Belgium to help a group of people who were doing a similar thing over there. I started doing occasional work in a massive music shop, demonstrating the Gibson Guitar Synthesiser.

It was then that I realised that what I really wanted to do was get a band together.'

So he got in touch with a couple of friends who were living in London, and asked if they wanted to spend a few months in Belgium getting things together. They did, and began the Stuart David Band. Stu chose his middle name because at the time, Ken, who was both manager and mentor, reckoned that David was a much better sounding surname than Garrard.

'I was young and naive so I did whatever I was told.'

The band rehearsed every day and wrote songs - the format of Stu on guitars and vocals seeming to work well with Johnny Martin on bass and Darren Springer on drums. When they were ready, they returned from the safety of the continent to try their hand at touring. They visited groups of friends they had up and down the country, playing in pubs and halls. The tour was a success and they added Richard Causon on keyboards, and (reflecting a much more democratic vibe) changed their name to The Treasure Park.

The band spent a further 18 months working hard. They graduated from the pub to the club circuit that was the heart of the London music scene at the time.

'We used to go to these 'Pay to Play' venues: you'd pay £50 for sound and lights, get a few mates along, and if you were lucky you might get a slice of the ticket sales. They were great times though; going out in front of a cold audience meant you either shied away or played the best you could.'

Towards the end of the band's life they added a lead singer, a New Zealander called David Morris. Together, the five were trying to be a 'proper band', playing venues like the Marquee and The Borderline. Songs carried a Christian influence, but the gigs were aiming to be a part of the mainstream music scene.

'One of my problems is that I'm an eternal optimist. I really believed that five blokes could all think the same thing, all go in the same musical direction. Once I saw the cracks beginning to appear, I thought that meant the band was destined to fail, so I finished it. In one sense it was probably one of the worst things I've ever done relationally. In another sense it was a good thing, as it led me on to new experiences. I learnt a lot of lessons at that time.'

Stu went back to the church for a period, writing songs that could be sung during the service.

'Then I had one of the best musical experiences ever. I started playing for this Reggae artist from Nigeria called Ben Okafor. There was Terl Bryant on drums and Eddie Branch on bass. I loved the space in the music, and really got off on the vibe of playing the same chord for ten minutes.'

When the band finished, Stu received offers to tour with some up-and-coming mainstream bands. Because of a clash of dates he had to turn both down: one with an up and coming band called JJ, another with ex Bauhaus frontman, Pete Murphy.

'I was gutted that I couldn't do the tours; getting out there was exactly what I had wanted to do for ages.'

Instead, Stu and Karen pursued a hunch that led them and their first daughter, Kaitlyn, to Kettering, south of Birmingham. Seeing it as a transitional time, Stu took a job as music co-ordinator for a group of churches. The job allowed him plenty of time to take up offers of session work with many of the names on the Christian scene: Kevin Prosch, Noel Richards. For a time Stu was laying down the guitar tracks on almost every album that was being produced around the scene. It wasn't long before a friend who was producing a new band's tape asked him if he would be able to come to Littlehampton for the week's recording. A family holiday meant that this was another gig he had to turn down. Unlike before though, this would not be the last he would hear of it.

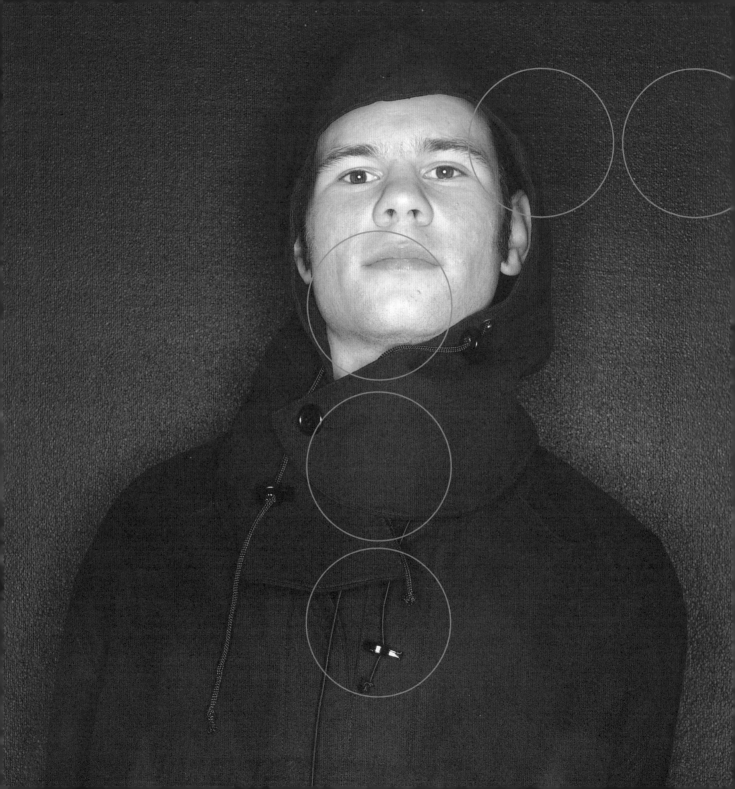

Jon

For Jon Thatcher, being a part of Delirious? had almost happened long before he had ever played bass with them. His three older sisters - Becca, Sarah and Anna - had each married guys from church - Tim, Stew and Martin - who were the first to form the band. Jon spent many hours listening to his extended family discuss the band, its future and its aims. It would take three years until he was finally in.

Jon was born in 1976. The presence of three older sisters ensured that his home was always busy and loud. His parents had set the church up a few years before, and their house was a focus for meetings with all sorts of people. A naturally quiet person, Jon escaped the chaos by spending time in his room. However, this didn't mean hours of Space Invaders. From the start he preferred the more creative kind of hobbies. Painting, writing and listening to music were part of Jon's solution to boredom.

'When you'd go downstairs and realise that you didn't know anyone, going sheepishly back upstairs was always the best thing to do.'

Not that this made Jon unhappy; the sense of freedom, of being able to look after himself, was very appealing. 'I suppose it started by being the youngest. My parents had lightened up a bit, had stopped being quite so strict. I just slipped through the net.'

And so Jon was brought up aware of his own individuality. Until the birth of Ben (his younger brother) in 1988, he was the only boy in a sea of girls. At school he became the pupil that got along with almost everyone, but who didn't settle down into any of the groups.

'I enjoyed school. I was always the guy that got the Effort prizes: I was never very academic, but I never put a foot out of line.'

Each report card trotted out the same line: 'Jonathan is a

quiet and conscientious member of the group and a pleasure to teach'. Whereas others found ways to express themselves through rebellion, Jon's methods were far more subtle. When the option came for people to fall into either the Indie-kid or Raver category, Jon had found an alternative hobby.

'I used to love coming home, changing out of my school uniform and going out on my deck with the others till eleven at night. You'd wonder where the time went.'

In many ways, skateboarding was a strange choice for Jon: being into it meant joining a group of people who were dressing in a similar way, adopting an accepted language, and listening to a certain range of music. Skate culture thrived on being different from the majority, by being a similar minority. Perhaps this time of being accepted by a big group was necessary for Jon; perhaps it was his own teenage rebellion - breaking away by becoming part of a group.

Unlike Martin, Jon never found that his faith caused conflict at school. Classmates were already confused by his interest in art and bands they had never heard of. What difference did one more side to Jon Thatcher make?

Jon's musical history starts back in his bedroom, listening to Nik Kershaw, Run DMC and other mid-eighties legends. Having been introduced to the bass by his Uncle, Jon knew from an early age that it was the intrument for him. But, being a particularly small ten-year-old, he had to wait for a couple of years before he was big enough to pick up the bass. 'When I was 13 I split my time between skating on the street and playing bass in damp garages throughout Littlehampton.'

Once Jon had got the basics down, he entered a phase in his life when he tried to get in as many bands as was physically possible. For the second half of his teens he supplied the low end for Funk groups, Thrash groups,

Rockers, Grungers and Acid Jazzers. Gigs took place in school halls while nervous teachers complained about the volume and not being able to hear the words. Among the star turns was one that stood out from the rest. 'Disneyland Freakshow' was a psychotic cocktail of kitsch Garage Rock and bizarre lyrics from Jon's 'alternative' sub-conscious. Jon wore a dress on stage.

After A Levels (Art and Philosophy) Jon pursued his interest in art by leaving school and starting a Foundation Course in Art and Design, specialising in photography and graphic design. By now Stew was his brother-in-law, and his career as a graphic designer was going well. Spending time together inspired Jon, as he saw ways of translating creative thought onto printed paper.

It was during this year that the 17-year-old Jon was asked by his brothers-in-law to play with their band. The search for a permanent bass player had been ongoing ever since the band started, and over the years more than seven musicians had tried and taken the role. They never lasted very long. Despite his frantic band-joining at school, Jon was the least experienced of all of them.

'Tim, Martin and Stew used to sit around the table at home, scratching their heads and wondering where they were going to get a bassist from. I don't think I was desperate to be asked: I wasn't totally sure if I liked the music at the time.'

By the time he was asked, saying no to being in a band was not something Jon ever did. The first gig was a local one, and they had been stood up by their bassist with just hours to go. In the end it went well, and Jon was asked to join them on a gig the following week in Maidstone, Kent.

'It was a nerve-racking experience: getting out in front of a crowd, playing someone else's songs. I did get paid for it, which was even more unusual for me.'

A formal invitation never followed; Jon was just asked if he could make gigs as they came about. It was clear that Jon's part in the band was secure when he was asked to play on one of the tapes. This was not his first time in the studio, as in 1995 Stu G had asked him to play on his own six-song tape, 'Have You Heard?'. The session was Jon's big break: Stu G took a gamble on the inexperienced youngster. His hunch paid off, as Jon came up with some inspired parts that raised a few eyebrows in the bass-playing community.

'I had just started a degree course in Design at the local college. One of the reasons I chose it was that it was near home, and the tutor had told me early on that if I ever needed time off for the band, he would do whatever he could to help. It turned out he was a bass player too, so I felt confident that he was on my side.

'So the first week I found out about needing a week off for recording. I went into his office and told him that the studio had been booked for three weeks' time, but I would make up all the hours I missed.'

Jon was sure his tutor was going to cut him some slack, but instead the tutor told him it was impossible. 'You can either be in a band,' he said, 'or you can get yourself an education.'

'I was gutted. I was so keen to do the course, but the band was important too. I asked for some time to think about it and went home to talk it through with my parents. They told me that they were one hundred per cent behind me, whatever I did.'

The next day Jon quit. He was told that he was insane by his tutor, and walking home he began to wonder. This was in September; it was not until the following April that the rest of the band joined him by going full-time.

By this time Jon had found himself a girlfriend. True to form, Jon hadn't opted for the usual; instead he had gone for the exotic and looked far from home. Kristen Groblewski was a trainee actress from Bethlehem, Pennsylvania, whom he had met while taking children to the toilet at a conference when he was 15. This act appealed to Kristen and the two of them corresponded

occasionally over the following few years. After a visit from Jon one summer, Kristen decided to move over to England and enrol on a course closer to Littlehampton. By the time Jon and Kristen got engaged, the band were releasing singles into the charts.

Jonathan is a **quiet** and **conscientious** member of the group and a **pleasure to teach**

The Cutting Edge Days

By the time 1992 came around, Martin, Tim and Stew were busy talking. Music was on the menu, but so were a lot of topics: youth, boredom, hope and creativity. They were part of a church that was nurturing a history of being involved with its community. Years before, they had been holding meetings unlike any other; people who had never been to church were dropping in. Without knowing why, many of them reported that they had just felt drawn to the meetings. A few years down the line, the next generation were itching to be a part of their own thing; to set something up that would continue the tradition of being a relevant voice on the streets.

Together, the team (including Tim's wife, Becca) got round to thinking about what they should do. At that time the fashion was for multimedia events: slick presentations of the gospel welded to hi-tech visuals and low-fuss rules. Of the various events already up and running, 'Interface' in south-west London was regularly pulling in over 1000 teenagers. The team considered adopting the formula, but realised that what worked for a bunch of city-dwelling teens might have a different effect on more rural types. Added to that was the fact that each member of the team was more 'pub' than 'club', more Rock than Techno.

And so it came to pass that they decided to do what they felt they could do best: get a band together, have a bit of worship, throw in a quick talk to get everyone thinking, and leave the rest to brew on the night. They approached their pastor/father/father-in-law (David Thatcher) and told him of their plans. His response was simple but committed.

Within a month they had a name, a venue, a band and an event. The first Cutting Edge took place in October 1992 in the Angmering School drama studio. Becca introduced it from the balcony at the back, and Tim, Martin and Stew played through a set made up of various songs by Martin ('Lord You Have My Heart' and 'The Crucible For Silver'), Kevin Prosch ('Banner' and 'Shout To The Lord') and Noel Richards ('There's Power In The Name Of Jesus').

Martin had only just joined the church, and carried with him many of the mannerisms picked up over previous years. He was never too keen on interrupting the flow of the songs with talk. Part of this came from his background, but part was because of nerves.

'I was a wreck,' Martin says. 'Talking through a microphone to a whole bunch of people had me tongue-tied. I'd try and get a sentence together, but end up in such a state that we'd just start a song off to ease the embarrassment.'

For Tim and Stew, though, saying a few words between the songs was a vital part of leading the congregation. Over time, the two camps grew closer together, as Martin relaxed and the band began to form its own identity. For a couple of years, though, it was easy to see the differences between Tim's on-stage exuberance and Martin's sense of focus.

'After that first event,' says Tim, 'we went back home and dissected the meeting. We were desperate to find out what areas we could improve on.' For the team this became a regular part of each meeting, as important as the sound check. Years later, when the band would become its own entity, the post-event analysis would remain in place. Even at gigs today, the main aftershow event is more likely to be a big chat than wild partying. In these situations the strength of their friendships comes across, as they can be honest with one another to the point of being rude. Conversations can last for hours and spin off into discussions of contemporary culture, music and the future. Sometimes, though, Stu G does his impressions.

Seventy-five people turned up for the first Cutting Edge. The following month 150 were there. The numbers grew steadily until they reached 1000 in 1994. Before long the team had all got used to the constant searching for new venues. Each time a new one was discovered their

hampton Beach Green 07.96

reactions were a mash of relief that it had been found, awe that it could be more than half filled, and amusement that, one day, it too would become cramped. Even so, when the venues were new and baggy, the band made a point of setting up on the floor, about halfway up, in an attempt to make the event look less empty.

While Stew, Tim and Martin were the core of the band, they brought in others for the gigs. Over time, many bass players and guitarists filled in: some for longer than others. If Tim and Martin had either bassist or guitarist coming in to the studio around the date of a Cutting Edge event, they would be sure to book them in for a Monday morning session. To solve the problem of an early start to the week, they would suggest the musos arrive on Sunday. Booking them up in the diary, Tim would often let out a little 'Well I never' in surprise, as he saw by chance there was a gig on that night. In this way the Cutting Edge Band kept themselves well fed on quality musicians.

For a long time the band was a part of a larger story: Cutting Edge was an event, and it was only as the offers from gig promoters came in that the name Cutting Edge Band came into existence. The name wasn't even their idea: it came from those gig promoters who needed some way to refer to the band. Because of their connection with the event, it seemed that the name was the most obvious choice.

The band needed a name because they had decided to do a tape. There had never been a strategy for the events. As Stew says, 'We only ever took it from month to month. In between each event Martin would write a new song based on the theme of the meeting.'

By the time Easter 1993 had come around, Martin had written enough songs to make up their first tape. Tim's home studio had grown and was now resident in the ground floor of a building he had taken over. Together, he and Martin were working as engineer and producer for various local bands and Christian projects.

The idea of doing a tape themselves was a logical progression, and one that they knew would work: they only needed to sell 250 tapes to break even.

With the help of Andy Piercy - ex After The Fire frontman - as producer and a couple of session musicians providing bass and guitars, the first tape was recorded in a week. It was up to Stew to design a cover, and by June's Cutting Edge event, *Cutting Edge One* was on sale at the back of the hall. It took two weeks to sell out.

Stew's cover was simple, but that was not through a lack of inspiration. They didn't want to be seen as a band, and initially they talked long and hard about wanting to be perceived as faceless, letting the music speak for itself. This innocence matured in time, and later artwork did include band pictures, but in those early days the band were like any other: bright eyed and full of plans to revolutionise the world. The cover for the first tape was a bold yellow with the only text on it being 'Cutting Edge - songs by Martin Smith'. In their attempt to play down the band, they accidentally built things up in a way they hadn't wanted. For years people would refer to them as Martin Smith and Band, Cutting Edge with Martin Smith or The Martin Smith Experience. It took a long time to change people's minds.

And so this was the pattern for a while: the events grew and the tapes sold. Tim would spend the Friday afternoon before the event driving to various companies to pick up equipment. It was a true underground following: at first you could only buy the tapes at the event. Across the country people wondered who Martin Smith was, and did he look anything like his brother Stewart? As the news spread, so the demand increased. Invitations to take the band to other youth events became more frequent. By the summer of 1994 the band had recorded another tape (*Cutting Edge Two*) and were regularly playing to crowds of over 1000.

Calling it an 'underground thing' touches on the heart of the band's success: news about them spread not through clever marketing campaigns, but by word of mouth. And those mouths that passed the information on helped to move the band into new areas. As the band spent more time playing around the country, so they began to realise things about Littlehampton. As their home and base for the Cutting Edge events it would always be a special place for them. At the same time, the idea of travelling to different places, taking their message and music with them, was becoming more appealing. Perhaps it was at these times - driving through the night to play in a school hall in the middle of nowhere - that the boys began to feel like a band.

During Easter 1995 the band went into the studio to record their third tape. Stu G had moved down in the previous months and was now a fully signed-up member of the band. His influence can be heard, particularly in the thunderous 'I'm Not Ashamed' and the groove-led 'I've Found Jesus'. But the track that stands out the most is the spiritual battering-ram 'Did You Feel The Mountains Tremble?'

'It came,' according to Stew, 'soon after we had moved into a new venue. Although we were really pleased to be in this huge sports hall, we knew that we wanted things to reach much further than the meetings.'

The venue in question was one of Littlehampton's few sports halls. At the same time, they had also responded to an invitation from a guy in Southampton called Billy Kennedy. Billy was keen to set up a Cutting Edge event in his home town, and asked whether the band would be a part of the event. They were well up for it, and were soon turning up for another CE regular in Portsmouth. At all three venues 'Mountains' went down a treat.

For the months that followed the song's release, people jumped on board with the chorus ('Open up the doors and let the music play') like they had never done before. Here was another defining moment in the life of the band: a song had arrived that was musically extremely powerful, lyrically poetic, and spiritually focused on the world beyond the church. In time, more songs would take on board these characteristics, as the vision began to come into focus. 'Mountains' soon spread, and before long the band were regularly getting letters from people around the world telling of how much the song meant to them. 'It was amazing,' says Martin, 'to see the song that was written for Cutting Edge being sung around the world.'

As a wannabe guitar player, the band took pity on me at an event in the summer of 1995. Stu G was off playing with the band I sometimes played with, and Martin, Stew and Tim agreed to having two of our singers and myself play with them for the week. Martin had just returned from his honeymoon when I visited him for a pre-event rehearsal. Sitting nervously in his flat I listened as he played through some new songs, 'Find Me In The River', 'Oh Lead Me' and 'Did You Feel The Mountains Tremble?'. He told me how, when he was writing 'Mountains', he had 'heard' the cheers that have accompanied the end of the verses ever since. Playing it through on acoustic guitars was an interesting experience, but it wasn't until we played it with the rest of the band that my shaking spine was the result of something other than nerves. It was without doubt one of the strangest and best experiences I have ever had with a guitar: like riding alongside a herd of manic and wild horses. The way I played there was no finesse or class, but to everyone in the room the song was pure dynamite.

By the summer of 1995 the band were in incredible demand: they were playing every weekend (as well as doing their own full-time jobs in the week) and notched up a summer audience of over 16000 people. Jon's informal apprenticeship had been going for a few months, and by now he had graduated to full-time status.

At the end of August Martin was producing the live album for an event based in Lincoln, called 'Grapevine'. The birth of Stew and Sarah Smith's first child, Abi, had happened while he was away, and he (along with Anna and Jon, who he had gone to visit) was keen to get back as soon as he could. They decided to drive the 230 miles back home once the event was over.

At 2.34am, just half a mile from home, Martin fell asleep at the wheel. He awoke after the car crashed into a brick wall. He was sitting with the dashboard on his legs.

Whereas Anna and Jon escaped with relatively minor injuries, Martin was trapped in the car for over an hour and a half while the rescue services tried to cut him free from the wreckage. At first Martin thought that he had lost his legs. 'I can remember looking at my hands and thinking, "at least I can still play". I can also remember a lot of pain.'

The two weeks that he spent in hospital turned out to be a key point in the Delirious? story. Martin read Bill Flannagan's *U2 At the End of the World* and was given a tape of the band speaking in the early '80s about their lives.

'I knew that God was speaking to me. I started to think about what I wanted to do with my life. Was my aim to earn good money as a producer, or do what I was made for and make music? I felt that God was telling me to get out there and raise the flag for this generation. "OK," I thought, "I don't care about the immediate hurdles or financial risk: I feel like I've been given a second chance and I'm going to take it.".'

Once out of hospital, Martin put his idea to the other four band members. He suggested they all give up their jobs and take a wage from the band's gigs and merchandise sales. As if the decision wasn't hard enough, the fact that four out of five of the band were related to one another by marriage introduced an extra dimension to the discussions. They decided that they would have three months in which to make up their minds.

The months that followed were tense and a true test of all their friendships. As the discussions progressed, the topics widened: everything was analysed, from the impact on the families to the motivations for 'success'. Each person had something to lose, although for some the decision took longer. Stu G, for example, had been waiting all his life to be in a band that really made it; giving up being a part-time electrician was no great sacrifice. Stew, on the other hand, was confused about how he saw himself: was he a designer or a drummer? Having worked hard on it for a few years, his business was taking off in the way he had always hoped it would. Going full-time with the band meant more than just a drop in income; it meant trading a certain future for one that was full of risks. At the age of 19, getting paid for being a full-time musician was a pretty good deal for Jon, although his decision was not taken without considering what sort of future he might have if the band didn't quite make it as they all hoped. For Tim, with Martin ready to quit his career as a producer, his studio would lose an important asset. Still, the studio had grown into a success of its own, and giving it up meant leaving behind a certain future. Although it had been Martin who had initially suggested going full-time, he had sacrifices to consider too. By the time of his accident he was the most sought-after producer on the Christian scene. Who knows what the future could have held?

Once time was up the decision was unanimous: they would all do it. In the three months that followed, everyone got on with the job of winding down their businesses and helping to set up their own record label, Furious? Records. The demand for Cutting Edge tapes and CDs was so great that they were already employing someone to process the orders which came from punters and bookshops in the UK, the rest of Europe and beyond.

But before all this, they sneaked in one last musical gem. It was to be the final chapter in the Cutting Edge thriller. *Cutting Edge Fore* brooded, popped and groaned its way from the studio out to people's homes. Instead of the usual six tracks, there were seven. From the looped-groove of 'Louder Than The Radio' through the musical maturity of 'When All Around Has Fallen' to the polished power of 'All I Want Is You' and the raw, blood-soaked passion of 'Obsession'. It was a corker.

Throughout it can be heard the voice of a post-accident Martin. Before the crash he sang about happiness and joy. August 30th taught him about pain and suffering. 'When you've been crushed to pieces' sometimes all that you can do is 'rest your weary head'. *Cutting Edge Fore* marked a period of surgery: it was only in recovery that they realised quite how much had changed. The band changed their name to Delirious?: they were not a grown-up version of Cutting Edge - they had been born again.

Sheffield 10.96

"I feel like I've been given a second chance and I'm going to take it"

Littlehampton 07.96

The Delirious? Girls

Focusing on the business side of things - the track from pop-ambition to reality - is all well and good, but it leaves out a part of the Delirious? story that is as important to where they are today as how they first met. The bit we've been missing is, of course, the chicks. Not that this is going to be a chapter detailing the hazy recollections of various Sues, Vickis and Natalies. Instead I find myself taking iced tea with five of them: Karen, Becca, Sarah, Anna and Kristen.

There's something innocent and 'teen' about the way people are referred to around Furious?. The band are always 'the boys' and their wives are 'the girls'. This is perhaps a hangover from when they first met and started to get married. In the eighties and early nineties the boys really were boys: they were fresh out of their teens - or in Jon's case, just about to go into them - and were just beginning their individual journeys. Today, they seem calm and assured, confident as they progress from one phase to another. At airports Delirious? always seem calm and assured, with matching luggage.

But in those dating days there was none of the polish we see today. When Becca first met Tim she was told by her future husband that her trousers 'looked like a pair of curtains'. Sarah first thought Stew was 'boring.' Anna first noticed that Martin's suit was way too big and his buttons were done up the wrong way. After an initial meeting with Stu G, Karen had forgotten all about him when he called her to arrange a date. Kristen first met Jon when he was taking children to the toilet at a conference. It seems his toilet escorting was a regular occurrence because he didn't enjoy the talks.

So you see, these ladies are no gold-diggers, seeking a free ride on the back of someone else's success. From those first meetings it seems they would have been hard pushed to imagine their respective boys as ending up as anything other than social odd balls. In many ways they did - forming a Christian rock band (a contradiction in terms,

according to the all-wise British music press) - but it is clear that Stew, Tim, Jon, Stu G and Martin have all come a long way. Those nervous first meetings flourished and became something special. Over the years everything has grown: the relationships, the work of the band, and the expectations for the future. The girls have played as key a role in the growth of the band as they have in the growth of their marriages. Here's how.

The Relationships

Stu G and Karen

Theirs was the first. Meeting in a pub in Ipswich, Stu G said 'hello' and that was it. Days later he called her for a date, and once she remembered who he was she said 'yes', and that was it. They married in 1984, had their first daughter, Kaitlyn, in 1990, and their second, Eden, in 1994. Stu G has the most authentic Rock Pedigree - remember all those gigs in seedy London venues? - and in Karen he has the most Rock of wives. Karen is (according to Becca) 'up for anything': whatever the plan, however long the tour or late the session, Karen is happy. 'I just love it when he's playing because that's when he's happiest.'

Tim and Becca

OK, so the trouser analysis from Tim wasn't the smartest opening move he could have made, but things got better. Despite a four-and-a-half year age gap, the two of them got it together after they both worked on a team at the Christian conference, Spring Harvest. 'I'm a bit slow, really,' says Mrs Jupp, 'and it took me a long time to come round to the idea of getting married.' Eventually she did come round and the two were married in 1990. Rosie, their first daughter, was born in 1994, Harry then followed in 1996, and Milly arrived in 1998. The early months of their marriage were spent with Becca, Stew, Tim and

Martin, getting increasingly excited about what they might be able to set up for the local young people.

Stew and Sarah

Her older sister, Becca, was already going out with Tim when Sarah met Stew at church. Again it was working on a team together at Spring Harvest that brought them together, and like all the girls, Sarah married when she was 20. She quit her job as a nurse when they had their first child, Abi, in 1996. Along with Tim and Becca, Stew and Sarah are the biggest defenders of their time against the pressures of touring and promotions. Making the decision to go full-time took them the longest of all.

Martin and Anna

They first met at Tim and Becca's wedding, after which Anna summed up her future husband with the words 'nice voice, bad suit'. When Martin moved from Eastbourne to Littlehampton he stayed with Anna and her family, but offered to move out on the second day when he realised he wanted to marry their youngest daughter. They let him stay and Anna concentrated on setting up her own nursery while Martin settled into the church and into his job as producer. Having married within a couple of years, the two of them had their first child, Elle-Anna, in 1997.

Jon and Kristen

The last to marry, in 1997, and the first to decorate their home with aliens and Elvis memorabilia. The relationship stalled at the pen-pal stage for years, with the frequency of correspondence between Littlehampton and Bethlehem, Pennsylvania, depending on whether one of them was seeing someone else. Eventually, after a particularly long break in letters and phone calls, Kristen was watching the movie 'Green Card' and started thinking about the strange little Englishman she had met years before. She called him,

he visited her that summer and, after a few weeks, they decided to give it a go. Kristen took a year out from studying drama at university and moved to England. They married within 18 months.

The Event

There are many people who can claim to have had a hand in the formation of the Cutting Edge events; there are also many occasions and places that inspired each person. For Martin, travelling to California and meeting Kevin Prosch was a catalyst. Stew and Becca were inspired by what they had seen at ground level in the town itself, through their roles as the church's youth leaders. For others, early visits to other events were enough to start thoughts about something similar occurring in Littlehampton. The point is that the Cutting Edge event had many champions in the early days.

Becca counts a meeting with Martin at - guess where? - Spring Harvest as a key growth point for her thoughts about providing for the locals. 'I felt shaky all over - it was one of the most prophetic conversations I've ever had.' Martin was telling her, as well as Anna, about his thoughts on worship: how it could be life-changing, intimate and, most of all, powerful.

Becca and Stew took on the job of heading up the event, but many more felt as though they owned it. David and Heather Thatcher - pastors and parents - housed not only Anna (who was dancing at the event) and Sarah (who was involved with the youth work) but Martin, Jon and Ben (their youngest). Their house became a focal point for discussion about the event: after each one, all the players would retire to the Thatcher house for cheese on toast and vicious analysis of the evening's activities.

The early events didn't hold many clues about the future success that it would enjoy. According to Anna, 'We knew it was exciting but no-one thought the numbers would explode. It was just a natural meeting that gradually got bigger. We probably prayed that loads of people would

come along, but it still blew our minds when they actually did.'

When Karen and Stu G joined in, the meetings had been going on for a little over a year. At first, Stu G came down on his own to play, but once Karen had heard the first tape, she played little else while she was at home. Soon the whole Garrard family was making the trip down for the weekend, staying with Tim and Becca, with Kaitlyn sleeping in her dad's guitar case while he played on Sunday evening.

The team always tried to do things differently: talks were given from the back of the hall and meetings were approached less as a lecture and more as an opportunity for people to meet with God for themselves. This was one of a few factors that combined to make the event feel like the work of a whole team. The band were rarely seen as separate to the rest of the event, although as time progressed and they started to record their mini-albums people began to differentiate between the two. In a strange way then, bearing in mind the involvement the girls had with Cutting Edge, they too were part of the birth of the band.

The Decision

As well as being largely responsible for the band's beginnings, the girls also played key roles in the progression from one stage to the next. The major step I have in mind is the decision to go full-time. The decisions that the families had to make were different for each of them: some were made quickly, some slowly.

Karen and Stu G made their decision first. 'The only concern that I had,' says Karen, 'was money: but then again when we first moved to Littlehampton, Stu only had two weeks of work booked and everything worked out well in the end.'

Then came Becca and Tim. 'After four days of our honeymoon we had to come home because Tim had a gig.

He played loads for the first few years, but in the months running up to Martin's accident he had been at home much more.' With the studio going well, Tim had been less of a musician and more of a businessman. Making the change would mean a return to uncertainty and lots of

Anna summed up her future husband with the words 'nice voice, bad suit'

travel. 'I knew it would be difficult,' says Becca, 'especially with two young children, but I knew that this was what God was calling him to do. Whenever there's a new thing I usually struggle at first, but I will come round in time.'

Sarah and Stewart took the longest to decide. 'I had only ever thought of Stew as being a weekend drummer,' she says. 'It had never been his ambition to be a drummer, and at that time graphic design was fulfilling him.' There was plenty at stake for the Smiths: the business was going well, both financially and personally, and Abi had just been born. 'It was hard because Stew had missed out on all the discussions in the hospital about going full-time. He'd been with Abi and me at home, so things felt quite strange.'

The period of three months that had been declared The Waiting Time gradually became more tense. They were relating to one another as family, as friends, but also as business partners and guardians of a spiritual vision.

Although it had been Martin's idea, going full-time raised questions for Anna. 'At the time he made the decision, Martin was quite an emotional wreck. One day he'd be up, and the next he'd be feeling low. I didn't know what the drugs were doing and I wanted him to wait, to take things slowly.' But Martin was adamant, fired up by an experience that had taught him that life was a precious gift that should never be wasted. 'I felt strange as my husband had come up with this idea that was going to affect all these people. I didn't know how it would affect my relationship with my sisters.'

Eventually it all came good. Sarah and Stewart decided that they were in. 'At the end of the day,' says Sarah, 'you have to make your own decision. You can't blame Martin or anyone else if it doesn't work out; I just wanted Stew to be fulfilled.'

And so they navigated their way through what has been their hardest time so far. In the years that have followed, those principles have remained in place: when a new schedule is devised, a tour is planned, or a trip suggested, the families are consulted. That way it still feels like everyone is involved.

The Life

Life for the girls is a curious mixture of the great and the not so great. Ask them what the best thing about Delirious? is and they'll go into a ten-minute long rapture about how they love the fact that their husbands love what they do. 'It's amazing that they love what they do,' says Kristen. 'Even after two weeks away on tour, they get back and they're still talking to each other. They're best friends and they miss each other when they're apart.'

When the subject changes to what they find hard, the inevitable top of the list is travel. Certain rules have been laid down by everyone concerned: no trips are to be more than ten days long, and each trip is to be followed immediately by time off when the band get home. This cushioning helps, but being away from family will always be hard. Interestingly, the hardest times are not while the boys are actually away. According to Anna, 'The time when they're away is normally easy: you get into a routine. When he comes back, dumps his washing down and needs some time to recover from the hard work of a trip, then that can be difficult.'

'Often,' says Kristen, 'when they come back they need their space: they've been stuck on a bus with ten other blokes for a fortnight and they need to relax. Then it can be hard. You wonder whether they've missed you.'

'I find the day before they go the hardest,' says Sarah. 'There's this pressure on you both to have a lovely day and spend 'quality time' together. At the same time you're getting ready to be all independent when they're gone.'

For each of the girls, church is as important to them as it is to their husbands, but it is also capable of throwing up the odd awkward situation. 'It's funny,' says Kristen, 'as some people there want to know exactly what's going on with them, while others get sick of hearing about it.'

When it comes to discussing the band at church, there is a kind of embarrassment/pride mixture. 'I'd rather not talk about it,' says Sarah.

'We feel so privileged...,' says Becca.

'And because of that we go out of our way to play it down,' says Kristen.

'I think,' says Karen, 'that is where a lot of our unity comes from: the fact that we all feel the same.'

'In a way, though, it can isolate you,' says Anna, 'as not everyone understands the relationships between us.'

And so their bond seems strong. Clearly, as three sisters there is a level of trust and openness that is important, but as a five they support one another too. For Kristen and Karen, settling in took some time.

'Stu and I had come from a church that had split,' says Karen, 'and it took me a long time to trust people again. Everybody knew Stu, and I was seven months pregnant when we arrived, so I couldn't get to many things. It was hard then, and it took me a couple of years to really feel at home here.'

'I didn't hold it against either Jon or the band,' says Kristen, 'but at times in the first few months that I was here I felt like I was the one who was making the big sacrifice: leaving my home, my country, my church and my friends. Now I love it here - even though I do want to go back and live there some day. The support I have over here is incredible, though.'

Another issue raised by the travel is the bizarre fact that, as Kristen puts it, 'There can be tens of thousands of people who know more about what he's just been doing than I do.' The irony of carrying out the domestic chores while her husband is out playing the rock 'n' roll game is not lost on Sarah. 'Sometimes I give myself a round of applause when I've put Abi to bed. If he gets some, why shouldn't I?'

For Anna, the fact that she is happy for her husband to travel so much is a sign that what he does is right. 'It must be God - why on earth would you let your husband go off all the time?'

If there is one area that is difficult, it is the children. Karen and Stu's two are older and have always known that their dad travels. Many of the others have had to get used to it quickly. 'We've chosen the life,' says Becca, 'but our children haven't.' At times the children have found their fathers' work difficult, 'But how many kids have their dads around to take them to school sometimes?' says Karen. It seems that with the negatives come the positives.

'I almost think that it's a privilege,' says Anna, 'for me to let Elle know that sometimes we have to make sacrifices: sometimes Daddy isn't there when she wants him.'

As the afternoon winds up and the tapes run out, it's time for one last chance for the Delirious? girls to have their say.

'There's been lots of talk about them selling out,' begins Becca, 'but we are totally on their case. We are always asking them why they're doing certain things, and there are lots of other people keeping an eye out too.'

'I do find it hard,' continues Kristen, 'when I've been to so many gigs and heard so many people cheer when they hear about the next single or mainstream release, only to hear that people are unhappy and critical as soon as the guys do something that looks vaguely secular. They're not selling out. They're really great guys and they're trying really hard to follow what God says.'

There's been lots of talk about them **selling out**,' begins Becca, **but we are totally on their case**. *We are always asking them why they're doing certain things,* and there are lots of other people keeping an eye out too

Tim on Stew

WHAT DO YOU ADMIRE ABOUT STEW?

His determination to pursue excellence in what we do. He's got a bit of a nerve when it comes to suggesting new ideas and directions. I admire his designs - the way that he always tries to make them unique. Without his musical and design skills we would have been like many other bands. As it is, he makes sure that we're never put in a box. He's very important to the way the band works as he's a team player.

HAS HE CHANGED SINCE YOU'VE KNOWN HIM?

We've all had to change. Stew comes from a background where he ran his own business and called the shots, but now as part of a team we've learnt that things don't always go the way we want.

WHAT WERE YOUR FIRST IMPRESSIONS OF STEW?

I remember being totally impressed by the fact that he'd been playing with bands in pubs. I felt a bit intimidated by this 'cos that seemed like real music, much better than playing in churches as I was.

WHEN HE'S STRESSED, WHAT DOES HE DO?

He doesn't like to be wrong, and when he's stressed he goes a bit quiet.

WHAT ABOUT WHEN HE'S HAPPY, HOW CAN YOU TELL WHEN HE'S IN A REALLY GOOD MOOD?

He's a silly boy, basically. He's quite an even kind of guy though; his mood stays pretty constant most of the time.

WHAT'S YOUR FAVOURITE BIT OF HIS PLAYING?

When he goes crazy at the end of 'Obsession'. There are moments when he really gets lost in it. I love to look over at him in 'Sanctify' when he's whacking his drums as hard as he possibly can: you can tell from his face that he's enjoying it.

Stew on Martin

WHAT DO YOU ADMIRE ABOUT MARTIN?

Lots. I admire his spirituality; he really wants to know God. Back in the early days, when we were getting to know each other, that was something that was very humble about him. He's also really determined about what he does, and as things have progressed he's seen more of the journey ahead of us. He has been key to making sure that we keep on track. The other thing I admire is that he's very honest, and if he sees things in your life that you need to address, he'll say it to you. It isn't always very nice, in fact, very often it's not very nice, but I do admire it. He does it because he wants the best for people.

Worthing 04.97 - shoot for *King of Fools* cover artwork

New England College, Ford, West Sussex 03.98 - interrupting early sessions for *Mezzamorphis*

Furious? offices 01.04.96 - the first day for the band as full time members of
Delirious? Jon wonders exactly what he has got himself into

London 06.98

Southampton 10.96 - Artwork for 'White Ribbon Day' single

Wembley 07.96 (above) and 07.97 (below) - note increased confidence

ittlehampton 06.97 - video shoot for 'Promise'

HAS HE CHANGED SINCE YOU'VE KNOWN HIM?

All those things I admire are things that have been there for a while, but they have definitely developed. He's found out more about himself and become more of a man.

HOW DOES HE SHOW WHEN HE'S STRESSED?

He goes quiet. He's a very thoughtful guy most of the time, but there are points when he can be a bit of a space cadet. He will retreat into himself, and be totally consumed inside. When we're in the studio and there are things to be done, he'll be totally focused to the point that you'll come in and say 'hello', and he won't even notice you're there. I admire that kind of focus, as well as being frustrated by it at the same time.

HOW CAN YOU TELL WHEN HE'S HAPPY?

Oh, it's obvious, he doesn't have any problems showing his emotions.

WHAT IS YOUR FAVOURITE BIT OF MARTIN'S SINGING OR PLAYING?

I like the fact that he's passionate about whatever he plays or sings. Lyrically he's great at capturing the way that everyone's feeling, putting it in a way that's both understandable and poetic - that's an incredible gift. 'Obsession' sums it up for me: it's full of analogies and is an amazing song to play live, it's passionate and explosive. For me that's exactly what Martin is.

Stu G on Tim

WHAT DO YOU ADMIRE ABOUT TIM?

I admire his ability to think about things in a very clear and business-like manner. He's quick to discern and is a very solid and faithful bloke. If he believes in something, he is virtually unshakeable, which is great - unless you disagree. He loves his family and has been key to us not spending too much time away. His clear thinking and determination really helped us strategise the first year of going full-time. Some people think he's a tough cookie, but if you look close you'll see a cuddly kiddy.

HAS HE CHANGED SINCE YOU'VE KNOWN HIM?

Yeah, he's got a bit more trendy, been on a diet, handed the managerial side to Tony and is a better keyboard player. Well done, Tim!

WHAT WERE YOUR FIRST IMPRESSIONS OF HIM WHEN YOU MET HIM AT THAT FORUM?

I remember him being really enthusiastic and I thought he needed a change of jumper - it was an eighties patterned woolly jumper.

WHAT YEAR WAS THAT?
1992.

HOW CAN YOU TELL WHEN TIM'S FEELING STRESSED?
Tim's emotions are pretty steady. It's easier to see when he's excited than stressed, although he can give it away by being a bit abrupt when he goes into brain overload.

HOW CAN YOU TELL WHEN HE'S FEELING HAPPY?
He's got this thing called a Christmas laugh, which doesn't only happen at Christmas but at any holiday time. He works hard and is very focused, but when we're not working he likes to let off steam.

WHAT'S YOUR FAVOURITE BIT OF TIM'S PLAYING?
For a start he's an outstanding pianist, and some of the lines that he's come up with over the years on the Cutting Edge things are really smart. I love what he did on 'Promise' with the Rhodesy sound. Some of the pads that he comes up with are really atmospheric. I think with all of us he's still developing. The best is definitely to come - watch this space.

Martin on Jon
Martin on Jon

WHAT DO YOU ADMIRE ABOUT JON?
His faithfulness: I think he'd do whatever God asked of him. I remember getting my first pair of DC trainers, and I didn't have a clue how to lace them up 'cos I'm an old boy. Jon said, 'Come on, give it here', and he did the laces in the cool way. There are many occasions where he does my laces for me symbolically. He's kept me on my toes with my writing, trying to push me into new stuff all the time. I think that he's always in your face a bit, saying, 'No, we've done that, we can't go back.' Being the youngest, he has a little bit more to put up with than the rest of us. People can see him growing up, and I think there's a lot of pressure sometimes. There would be no other bass player who could fit the job.

HOW HAS HE CHANGED SINCE YOU'VE KNOWN HIM?
He's become a little less intense and learnt more about his playing.

WHAT WERE YOUR FIRST IMPRESSIONS OF HIM?
When I first met Jon, he was only 14 and was a skate boy with a dodgy haircut. I liked his heart and his friendship with God.

HOW DOES HE SHOW WHEN HE'S STRESSED?
His top lip quivers and he looks like he's going to cry.

WHAT ABOUT WHEN HE'S HAPPY; HOW DOES HE SHOW THAT HE'S HAPPY?
He starts beating you up, punching you at the same time as saying 'I love you Mart'.

WHAT'S YOUR FAVOURITE BIT OF HIS PLAYING?
Verses three and four of 'Summer Of Love' are brilliant, and a real mark of someone creative. I think in 'King Of Fools' he is very inventive too.

Jon on Stu G

WHAT DO YOU ADMIRE ABOUT STU G?
He's very spontaneous and down to earth, but he's still got his head in the clouds at the same time. He's not satisfied with the obvious, and he's always wanting tomorrow, but at the same time he's content with what he's got today. He's a very positive guy. We joke that he's the oldest member, yet he's the youngest member too. He's 13 years older than me, but me and him probably get on the best in the band. He's got the kind of big brother thing but in a kind of totally unpatronising way.

HOW HAS HE CHANGED SINCE YOU'VE KNOWN HIM?
I don't think he's changed massively. He's more secure in himself, and we've got to the stage where we can be honest, whereas to start off with, I feel, in every relationship you play the roles.

HOW CAN YOU TELL WHEN STU G IS STRESSED?
He strokes his beard a lot and goes very quiet for a while.

HOW CAN YOU TELL WHEN HE'S HAPPY?
I think he's definitely a happy chappy. He's normally whistling, singing or dancing.

WHAT'S YOUR FAVOURITE BIT OF HIS PLAYING?
I like his part on 'King Of Fools'. He's got a real spacey sound on that. I like it when he rocks so hard that the big vein stands out on his head.

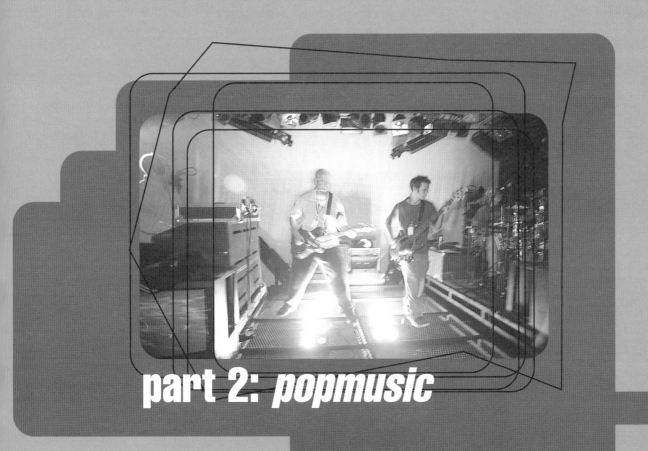

part 2: *popmusic*

delirious5 53

Christian vs Mainstream - The Story of 1997

Remember what we were saying about how Delirious? shouldn't really succeed? How, in theory, with all those musical influences, the schizoid offspring should have been kept under lock, key and heavy sedation? Well, prepare yourselves for even more confusion, as the history books open on the chapter marked 1997.

It was in this year that the band were more in control than before, yet the ride was the roughest ever. 1997 brought them more publicity than previous years, yet they felt like they were at the bottom of the class, lagging behind and struggling to catch up. It was the year of the first mainstream media coverage, of gigs with sprawling, anonymous crowds. There were ticket touts, bootleg merchandise, limos and fat lunches. And in the middle of all this were the high-points: the conversations and the new friends. OK, so playing in front of 50000 people isn't exactly torture, and being on national TV does have its plus points. Still, these aren't the things that the band hold dear. Throughout it all, they began to get a clearer idea of what they were here to do.

If ever they thought that their job was to be responsible, 1997 changed their minds.

'God,' said Stu G in the middle of the summer, 'doesn't need the charts. He doesn't need us to be releasing singles, trying to get him into the top 20.'

What? Had his fair-skin allowed in too many rays? Had the balding ginger lost it? It turned out that he hadn't; in fact he had very much found it. Delirious? began to see that what really mattered were the relationships. They began to see their role not as 'rent-a-ranter' - to be relied on to lay down the gospel good and heavy at any public event - but instead they developed the attitude they had used all along: 'If you like it, buy it'. Delirious? didn't want to make it into the charts because people felt duty-bound to put them there; they wanted to get there because they

made good music. On top of that, they were seeing that one of the main ways for them to influence people was not from the stage, but in front of the interviewer, chatting with the decision makers.

As the year progressed Delirious? began to picture themselves not as a complete evangelism strategy for lost souls, but as a band that sing about things they believe in. Their music may provide a focus for thoughts about God, but the greatest hope lay in the people themselves. God was still important, but the crowd were responsible for their own lives. Of all the songs that made it into their set, the one that always super-charged the atmosphere was 'HistoryMaker'. At the end of each gig the fans would leave singing to themselves, 'I'm going to be a historymaker in this land'. It wasn't the band that was going to make the difference, but them.

The year started with a miracle. The Cutting Edge event in the band's home town of Littlehampton had multiplied, and its clone had settled down for monthly meetings in the Southampton Central Hall. These were intense gigs, still saturated with the flavour of the old Cutting Edge style, despite the fact that the band had been going it alone for over nine months. At one of the first meetings of the year, over 1000 people were pressed in, hungry to see what would happen during the evening.

As usual it didn't take long for the walls to receive a generous coating of sweat. What was unusual for Martin, though, was the fact that in the afternoon he had stumbled across the thought that someone would turn up to the gig in a wheelchair. Considering the size of the crowd, this might not strike you as a particularly outstanding thought to be having in an afternoon. Still, something about it had caught Martin's attention.

'Once we were into the gig, that thought came back into my head,' said Martin. 'As soon as it returned I went up to

the mike and asked if anyone had come in a wheelchair that night. I thought I'd got away with it when no one replied, but from the back came a voice saying that her friend next to her was in a wheelchair. "Does she want to be healed?" I asked. The answer came back that she did.'

All along Martin was asking himself why he was doing it, but he managed to overcome his fears and get everyone to turn around and pray for the girl.

After a couple of minutes Martin shouted out, 'In the name of Jesus get up and walk!', thinking it sounded like the sort of thing you say to someone who you want to get up and walk. She did.

'On stage we were looking at each other, some were crying.' said Martin. 'We couldn't believe what we had seen. The girl was running around the hall, dancing and laughing. Later, when her dad came to pick her up, she ran into his arms while someone else carried the wheelchair to the car.

'It was the most incredible moment that I can remember: better than playing Wembley or any other gig we've done. It had an effect on us as a band, reminding us of what it was all about. We were just about to release our first single, and it felt like God was reminding us that these were the hits, the things to look forward to.'

The single that they were just about to release was 'White Ribbon Day'. Unusually for the band, the song had political roots: it was inspired by a news report from Northern Ireland that Martin had seen early on in 1996. The news story informed of new casualties in the area, but rounded off with news that a group of people had begun to talk of a day when peace would be lasting. Following in the footsteps of those who remembered their loved-ones at war by displaying yellow ribbons, these people adopted the white ribbon as a symbol of their hope. 'And as the violence increases,' went the report, 'the people pray for white ribbon day.'

Like a man who had not eaten for weeks, Martin consumed the words. It was exactly what he had been looking for - a way of expressing the beliefs and frustrations within that didn't rely on more traditional images. The song took a few days to write. He played it to the rest of the band. As with Obsession before, their reaction was strong.

'White Ribbon Day' got its first public performance at a gig at The King's Arms, Bedford, on March 6th, 1996. The atmosphere immediately changed. Almost supernaturally, something opened up within people and many began to weep. As the song finished, silence followed... Something had happened.

As they set down, a local businessman made directly for Martin and made him an offer: 'You have to record that song,' he said. The next day they received a cheque from him for £1000.

Soon the Christian scene hummed with the news of a song that made you weep, making for increased numbers at gigs. For some, hearing 'White Ribbon Day' was an intensely emotional occasion.

The band recorded it in May 1996, but the track stayed private for months. There were two reasons for this: one was because no one was sure what they should do with it, and the other was because, even if they were sure, the chances of anyone knowing how to go about doing whatever they decided to do with it were even slimmer.

Enter Tony Patoto. As a Christian working within the music industry (especially in the dance and 'novelty act' areas) Tony had kept a close eye on the band since 1993's *Cutting Edge One*. Just before 1997, after a few chance meetings, he and the band started to spend more time together as he gave them advice on what they should do next. Tony was Sales and Marketing Director at Total Records, the company who had agreed to distribute the band's material throughout the high-street shops. Six months later the advice wasn't free, as he had quit his job and joined Furious? Records full-time as the band's manager.

Together, the boys decided to release 'White Ribbon Day' as a single in the last week of February, 1997. The budget didn't allow for a video, and to keep it simple they took on one plugger to get the single played on national radio, and a press officer to get them in print. Among their own fans the band had been doing some long-term public relations work on the song. From the summer of 1996 through to the time of its release as a single, 'White Ribbon Day' occupied an important seat in the live set. Whenever it was played Martin said a few words about their plans to release it as a single. This led on to a few more words about their aims: to get out and be a part of the culture; to find a voice within the media to talk about the things they wanted to talk about; to take their fans with them.

The reaction was usually one of almost unanimous support. The fans were up for it, and it seemed that they had been waiting for a long time to find a band they could be proud of. Delirious? worked on a number of different levels: those who wanted to worship God through their music could do so. Some found the music an ideal way of letting friends know a little of what Christianity was about; some just liked the music. Releasing singles would help with all of these.

What the band were keen not to do was to try to get in the charts for the sake of it. They didn't want to spread the word that people ought to buy 'White Ribbon Day'. Instead they told people only to buy their singles if they liked the music.

For an unknown, unsigned band, choosing a debut single that contained a chorus that went 'Hallelujah, Hallelujah, Hallelujah' might not have been the most commercially sound move to make. Although the press officer managed a few clippings ('Bible band prays for stardom' wrote the *Daily Express*), radio support was even more reluctant.

The project was not a failure though. The fans managed to get the single to number 41 in the charts, missing the public profile of the Top 40 slot by just 141 sales. In fact, if the record stores had had a little more faith in the potential selling power of the band, they would have been well stocked, and the single would have entered the charts even higher. As it was, the shelves in high-street HMVs and Our Prices weren't exactly buckling under the weight of all the singles they were carrying. Within 24 hours of the single being available there was not one copy left unsold in the whole country. The next few days were a frantic struggle to get more CDs manufactured and out to the shops. At the end of the day, things just didn't move fast enough.

The fans were disappointed, but ready for another go. They knew that they could get their boys higher in the charts, if only the shops would sort it out.

A few months later they got their chance. The band decided to release a second single: the radio-bomb 'Deeper'. If ever there was a track that would get the airwaves nodding to the beat, it was this one. Playful, ballsy and brimming with groove, a new label had to be invented to describe it. And so chunky powerpop was born. 'Deeper' was on the way.

The single was due out in the middle of May, and the promotional wind-up started back in April. Furious? Records were handling the press themselves, but kept the national radio plugger from before, introducing another set of pluggers to take care of the regional radio stations.

The biggest boost to the 'Deeper' build-up came from the stores themselves. When 'White Ribbon Day' was out, they had been so amazed at the response of the fans, they vowed never to underestimate them again. This time they were stocking enough copies for double the sales.

Perhaps it was because the band were slightly better known, perhaps it was because 'Deeper' was a more

accessible song, but the promotional side of things began to fall into place. The boys made their first appearance on national kids' TV ('I bet Radiohead don't have to put up with this,' said Stew, as he was asked to take part in the Gunge Challenge). They told *The Independent on Sunday* how they were part of something that was here to stay (the paper called it 'God-rock'). Their video - directed by industry hot-property Steve Price - was shown on MTV.

The big day came, and despite a wall of silence from Radio One, they managed to break into the charts at number 20. The weeks that followed are slightly blurred. The single didn't stay in the charts for long, and the media coverage was wrapped up by the time 'Deeper' was at the 20 slot. It was confusing: as quickly as it had come, the attention vanished. Still, there was a lot of happiness at the time.

Not wanting to give up on a good thing, the band decided to keep going. When 'Deeper' was released, they had played and signed at a handful of HMV Megastores. These appearances felt important: when they were first suggested, many of us were amazed (this was the sort of thing that real pop stars did); when they were happening, they were a perfect symbol of the band's desire to get their music heard in the streets. In June they planned to repeat the tour, but this time to help promote their debut studio album, *King Of Fools*. Hopefully, the mainstream release of the album would place another feather in their cap when it entered the charts.

The decision to release their music through the high-street shops was a hard one to make. In the end it had bad financial consequences, but it was worth it to do what they wanted. For Stew and the others, it eventually came down to a matter of doing what they knew they had to do:

'Ninety-nine per cent of people buy their music from high-street stores. We have to get our stuff out there. Releasing singles is the way of getting yourself out there. Stores won't take your album unless they know you've got a following. That was all we wanted to do: give people who would have never had the opportunity to hear our music,

the ability to access it, hear it, be influenced by it, and hopefully enjoy it.'

What followed was a number 13 entry for the album, and a number 20 placing for the next single, July's guitar-fest, 'Promise'. With the single came a little more TV, press and radio, including an appearance on one of the Radio One Roadshows. It may have fulfilled the odd childhood dream, but it was still not enough to introduce the band to a big enough group of new fans to keep them in the charts for more than a couple of weeks.

By this time, the band were aware of the 'difficulty' some people in the media were having with 'that religious stuff'. In an interview with Melody Maker, Stew laid it on the line:

'I certainly am not one of those people who say, "If you're not a Christian I want nothing to do with you." You've got to discover it for yourself.'

It seemed to do the trick, and the journalist concluded that, 'Delirious? are not preaching. They don't see it as their role to convert everyone they meet, just that by behaving a certain way and having strong beliefs they can make a difference. And perhaps they will.'

There were a few experiences like this over the summer: conversations with people whose expectations of what a Christian band would be like were changed on impact. Although the mainstream success seemed a little shy in coming forward, the band began to see the potential offered by these friendships.

'Inevitably,' says Stu G, 'there are people who do not understand where we're coming from. Whether they're people in churches who think we're selling out to wanting to become rich and famous, or industry people thinking we're trying to use music to preach.'

'And people say,' continues Stew, 'that we're not doing a lot for the Christian faith through the singles. Those things are just a small part of what we do. Behind the scenes we might have a chat with some Radio One DJ or a magazine journalist; it's these people that are influencing the generation. By being ourselves we can leave them with an alternative perspective on Christianity.

'We will never ignore our beliefs,' he concludes. What Delirious? were finding out in 1997 was how to get them across.

Once 'Promise' had enjoyed its two-week stay in the charts, it was time for the band to take stock. The summer let the pace off slightly: there were a handful of big gigs, a trip to America to see how the future might develop, and a big fat holiday right in the middle.

As time passed the band began to realise just how much the previous few months' activities had cost them. Despite popular opinion, they had lost money on all of the singles, although the fan base was now at an impressive 25000. Each of the singles had achieved more sales than the last, although none of them had matched up to the initial high hopes. There was a sense of momentum about the singles that was hard to ignore. Like one of those fairground machines where you use the limp claw to try to pick up the tasteful gift, the temptation to throw some more money in and have another go was almost irresistible. It seemed as though they were so close, as if one more swift release would bring about the results.

This was the time of fast education. Just months earlier they had no concept of how the industry worked; by mid-summer they were beginning to wise up. After so many carrots had been dangled - so many promises of support slots, airplay and interviews that had come to nothing - the band decided to think long and hard before committing to another single.

In September Tony Patoto joined as manager, and negotiated his way to a substantial contract with Sparrow Records, America's leading Christian record label and a part of the EMI family. The band enjoyed a trip to Switzerland and returned home ready for the next step. They decided to have one last crack at mainstream success with 'Deeper'. Everyone had said that it was their most radio-friendly song, and more importantly, they had been told that one of the most influential men in the UK music industry had as good as promised to give it his full support if they re-released it. They were still keen to develop a platform for themselves, and the charts still looked like the best way of achieving that.

In early October the band went back into the studio to record some extra tracks for the single. Opinion was divided about the wisdom of re-releasing a single that the fans had supported so well before, but once they were committed, all were determined to make it the best-value single around. Two new songs were written (the bouncing 'Touch' and the brooding 'Summer of Love') and the pluggers booked.

The idea of doing a national tour had been floating around for some time, but right now seemed to be the best opportunity yet. The dates were tied in with the release of the single so as to give the radio stations maximum reason to play the song. The mood was optimistic.

As the tour got underway, the band travelled to each venue, stopping off at various radio stations along the way for an interview and a live song or two. The initial reaction was pleasing: the song was being picked up by a good number. The tour was doing well too, and gigs were selling out fairly regularly. At the last moment, though, things went wrong. The support that had been 'promised' vanished into thin air. Without a national profile, the single would do little more than be in and out of the charts in a fortnight. If it hadn't been for some astounding gigs, the mood would have been low.

In the end the Deeper EP entered the charts at number 36 and went straight out the following week. During the weeks that followed, the band and those at Furious? took stock of the situation. The d:tour had been a great success, the single hadn't. Yet singles are the only way to break a band into the mainstream. On the back of them comes (in

theory) media coverage. Without a single to promote, coverage is even harder to get.

Eventually, a number of thoughts emerged. First, was the decision about what to do next. Instead of feeling sorry for themselves, believing that they were being persecuted for their beliefs, Delirious? headed back to the studio.

'Maybe,' commented Martin, later, 'there was no conspiracy against us as a Christian band. Maybe the songs just weren't good enough.'

At an even later date Martin commented again, 'Maybe they were good enough, maybe it just wasn't the right time.' Months later no one is sure why the singles didn't fly quite as high as all had hoped. Theories come and go, but mostly people seem to be focusing on the next round - a new album and more releases.

Delirious? were determined to do well, and knew that they had some potentially great material inside them. According to Jon, the best way for the band to fulfil their aims is 'through the music. If the music's fantastic then people are going to want to hear it.'

1997 helped educate the band. They came out wiser, having learnt the inevitable lesson that things don't always go as planned.

The band also learnt about communication: reflecting the creator, they felt that there had to be other ways of expressing beliefs. Surely there must be a way of telling someone about God without using jargon that confuses and upsets people?

'I think,' says Martin, 'we so desperately want to communicate to people who don't know the lingo, who have never been inside the church bubble, that sometimes from within the bubble it looks like we've left. We've not left. We're taking it wherever it goes.'

In retrospect, the year went well, although not as well as they originally hoped. The singles didn't explode in the way they had hoped, introducing the band to a much wider audience. But for Stu G and the rest 'it was still a success'. For an unknown group, signed to an unknown (and relatively poor) label, to break into the charts four times in a year was quite an achievement.

'It was the fans that made it,' says Martin. 'They spend a lot of their money on us, and that does feel a bit weird, but it also makes us feel honoured. We try as hard as we can to make sure they get value for money, putting on good B sides and doing good shows on tour.'

If there were any regrets about the year, for Stu G it was being discounted by people simply because of Christianity. However, with the lessons learnt and the vision refined, Delirious? went back in the studio for the most part of 1998, recording their second album.

1997 had started with a warning to watch out for the real hits. Twelve months later there had been loads: great friendships formed with people from all over - security staff, caterers, journalists, box office staff, video directors, pluggers, roadies, reps and plenty more.

1997 helped educate the band They came out wiser, having learnt the inevitable lesson that things don't always go as planned

Guildford 05.97

Guildford 05.97 - packed in at the HMV

delirious? 61

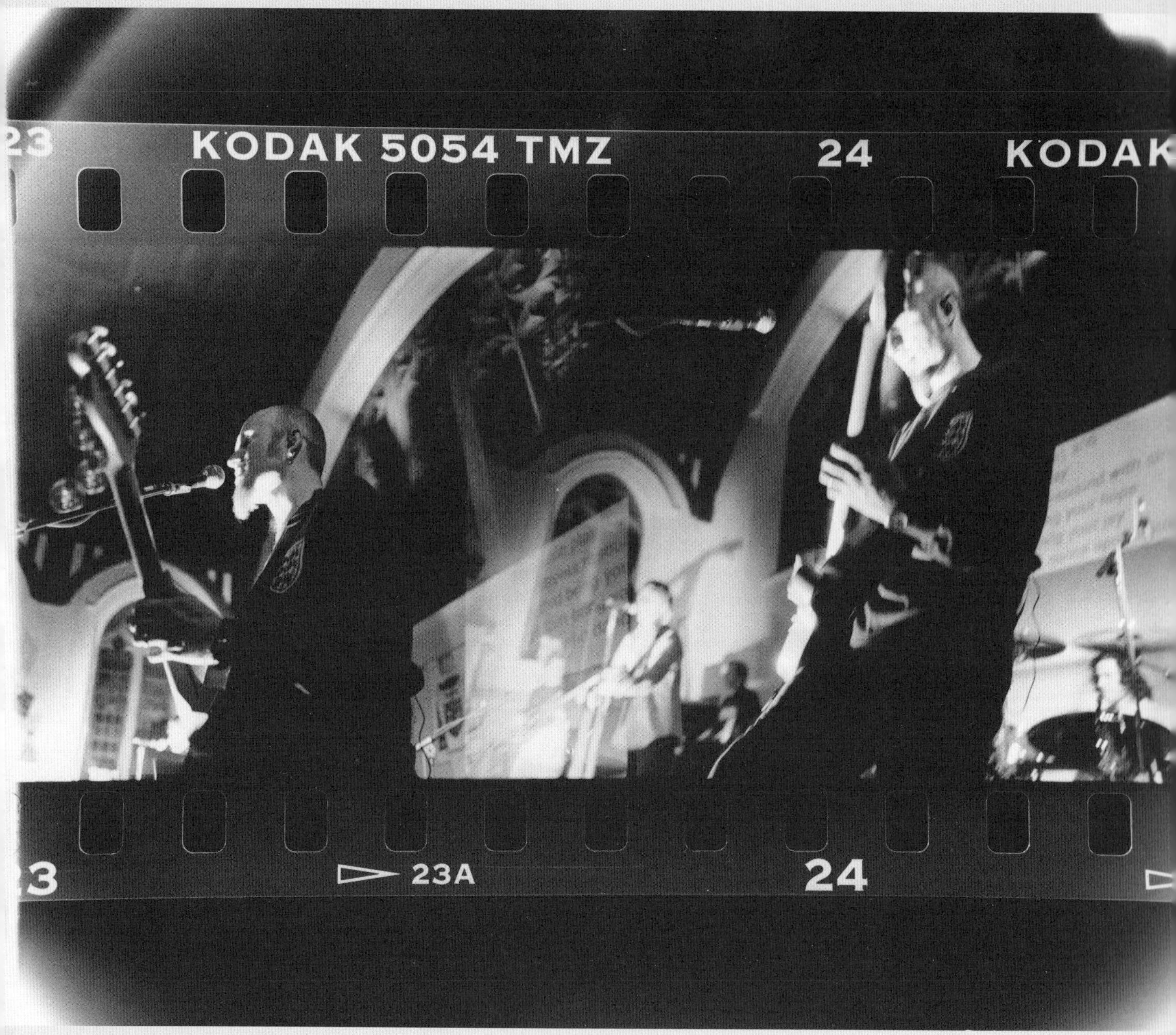
23
KODAK 5054 TMZ
24
KODAK
23
23A
24

Progress of the Music

Since 1993 the sound coming from the limbs and mouths of the Cutting Edge Band/Delirious? has progressed. Today's offerings can be heard wrestling for radio position alongside the big boys of the pop charts. Back in '93, if the music had made it onto the radio, chances are it would have been the Country Rock stations that would have picked it up. Not that in the early days they were bad, it's just that they've improved.

Take Martin, for example. Back in '94 he wouldn't dare go on stage without his mandolin, harmonica and telescope (don't ask). By the time '98 came around, no performance would be complete without his electric guitar and jester's hat. Progress, you see.

Or Stu G. There was a time when his solos sounded like auditions for a Budweiser advert: out came the bottleneck and the boy got busy with some good old country 'pickin' and 'slidin'. Now he is Man of Rock, delivering meaty solos that sound distinctly more Manchester than Memphis.

Over the years the others have caught up too: Jon has learnt to turn up the volume and play the lines that he hears in his head; Stew has quit the skippy shuffles of the country style, and Tim has delved deep into the bag of sounds that are atmospheric and great.

Time has been good to the band. Whereas most bands start with a very current sound and end up being labelled dated, Delirious? have gone the other way. In '92 they sounded like a poor relation to the early works of Deacon Blue or Texas. The '97 release of King Of Fools brought them into line with the rest of the UK music scene: Britpop had been and gone, and both had come out the other side. The band hadn't quite absorbed the sonic buzz and fizz of the dance culture, but Stu G's big guitars and Jon and Stew's cheeky rhythms signed them up alongside groups like Dodgy, Eels and other such acts.

But the journey from there to now hasn't been easy. Not only have they had to learn to work as a band, but they have had to remind themselves to compare their sound to what they hear in the charts, and not to what they hear in the church. At the same time, there is a feeling that they want to take their friends/fans in the church with them.

When Cutting Edge started, the combined musical experience of Tim, Stew and Martin was pretty limited. Stew and Martin had done pubs while Tim had stuck to the church. Cutting Edge was very much a church event, and there was no hint of rebellion in what they were doing. Early gigs did have a higher volume than other church events, but the overall sound was more church than chart. The boys were doing what they knew best.

At the time, most of them thought it sounded great. What they were doing was kind of unusual, but it was the reaction to the event that really got them thinking. For an event to grow so quickly was almost unheard of.

For the first three years of Cutting Edge, until the release of their third tape, it seemed as though musical progress was less important to the band. Later they would describe themselves as musicians, but back in the early days they all had other things to be getting on with.

Cutting Edge One and Two are, in retrospect, relatively similar. Both follow similar formats: slow numbers ending each side; less 'religious' tracks starting the second side of each tape. Guitar sounds are thin and the rhythms are skippy. The high-points are the slower numbers: the fragile honesty of 'Lord You Have My Heart' and the timeless intimacy of 'I Could Sing Of Your Love Forever'.

To Stu G the sound 'felt like the early days of a band. It was quite a jangly, beat sound, and I think that it really served the purpose of the events. It was an amazing starting place but we would sometimes talk about one day

when the music was being played on the radio, or the band was playing in a stadium.'

Opinions on the future of the band differed. When it was the three of them, Stew was in it because he liked drumming and wanted to put something on to stop the local kids from getting bored. For Tim, the biggest enthusiast of the lot of them - the band at times seemed invincible, ready to take on the world. Martin was too busy trying to get over his nerves to contemplate talking to tens of thousands of people at a time, although somewhere deep down was a belief that one day things would be big.

Stu G's arrival was important to the band's progress. Although he appeared on the second tape, it was not until the third that he played a major part in the overall sound. In the late eighties Stu G had been getting his head round the technical side of his instrument. He could play faster than most, and proved himself to be a fine player when he attended London's Guitar Institute. Joining Cutting Edge coincided with a new dawn in his playing technique.

'At the time I was really into *Pablo Honey*, the first Radiohead album. I know Cutting Edge sounds nothing like it, but that's how I wanted it to sound.'

Stu G left behind the frantic soloing of the former years, and worked on a more spacey, less technically ambitious sound.

'I just wanted to let the songs speak, to do whatever was best for them. Before that I used to try to cram in all my favourite licks into the solos.'

Listen carefully to the third tape and you can hear the change. Instead of the smooth, smiley sounds of the first two, *Cutting Edge Three* presents the listener with a more aggressive and emotive sound. Even during the tranquil closing moments of the last track, 'Find Me In The River', the rhythm picks up and Stu G's twitching sounds echo across the song.

The obvious change can be heard in the combustive 'I'm Not Ashamed'. This was the first time the band had ever 'done' Rock. The reaction at gigs proved they had done it well.

If Stu G was a major player in the third tape, then it was Martin's accident that co-produced the fourth. Musically, it's easy to hear the change in the tones and mood of tracks like 'You Split The Earth', 'When All Around Has Fallen', 'All I Want Is You' and 'Obsession'. It can also be heard in different ways in 'Louder Than The Radio'. It is a sound of a band who are inches away from radio play, the closest yet to the sound of the street. It is the sound of a pop group, for that is what they had decided to be.

There is one last element that frustrates the neat ending of the Cutting Edge years. As it stands, it all fits together neatly: they started out sounding like they'd just had tea with the vicar, and ended up sounding like they'd pierced his nipples. It seemed like the progress was smooth, all apart from one track: *Cutting Edge Fore*'s 'Shout To The North'.

'To be honest,' says Martin, 'that song doesn't really fit on the tape at all. We had just been through a really difficult church situation where a lot of people had left, and some of the leaders had parted company. The song just came out to encourage the people to keep looking outwards, not to get too introverted.'

Originally the plan had been to play it at church and leave it at that. However, the track went down well in the church, and Martin thought about putting the song on the next tape. The feel of the song - Riverdance with more guitars - was at odds with the rest of the tape. 'Whether putting it on was the right decision or not, who knows?' says Martin. Still, he has no real regrets.

After the final Cutting Edge tape was out, the band changed their name to Delirious? and started preparation for a full-length, live album. *Live and In The Can* was recorded throughout 1996, the year when they went full-time, gigging at least three times each week. When the

CD came out in the winter of that year it sold over 8000 copies within the first two weeks. Not great by today's standards, but virtually unheard of at the time.

As the band dropped the Cutting Edge name (one which they had begun to find slightly too self-proclaiming) there was more that had to change beneath the surface than just the name. Previously, with Martin as the principal writer and Andy Piercy as producer, there hadn't been a great deal of room for the others to 'steer the ship' in the studio. The six tracks for each tape used to be recorded within a week, again increasing pressure on the creative input from the others.

Once they had become Delirious?, the set-up was different. Perhaps the first test was when they went into the studio to record 'White Ribbon Day'. Having spent a day working out ideas, they were about to record the drum tracks, when Martin wondered out loud whether the song would be better a couple of beats slower. None of the others agreed, but the singer became more keen on the idea. Soon, he was sure of what he wanted, and so were the band. Although the atmosphere was friendly, it was clear that Martin would previously have expected to get his own way. From now on, that wouldn't necessarily be the case.

According to Martin, 'In the early days, when I used to write the songs in my bedroom, I would have a good idea of how I thought they should sound. Because I had some experience in the studio and I knew a bit more than the others about how to put records together, I did decide exactly how they came out. When we started on *King Of Fools* we knew that we would rise and fall together. I had to learn how to let go of a lot of things, and allow everybody to find their space in it.'

Challenges still come Martin's way, and to expect five years of ship-steering to evaporate quickly overnight would be unreasonable. For the others, it has taken time for them to get into the habit of being responsible for the Delirious? sound.

'That's why I've stayed quiet for a lot of the time,' says Jon. 'If I don't like a song and I haven't got any ideas for improving it, I end up just feeling frustrated.'

Stu G shares this sense of frustration, although for him it is caused by having too many ideas. When ambition clashes with experience...

'I feel like I'm banging my head against a brick wall. I know where I want to go, how I want things to sound, but I just don't have the ability and experience to make it happen.'

This frustration is often focused on lyrics, which Stu G finds hard because, according to him, he 'lacks poeticism'.

'We've grown out of the arty phase, having candles and joss sticks in the corner to help the vibe,' says Martin. 'The last time we did it was with 'What A Friend I've Found'. It was about one in the morning and all the lights were out. We had a couple of candles burning and every time I did a take I'd just end up lost in my own little world. Andy (Piercy) would be whispering down the headphones "are you all right in there?"

'After a while it becomes more of a job and you don't need the trinkets to make it work. I do remember recording the vocals for 'King Or Cripple', though. We had to be out of the studio within hours and I was still trying to get the vocal right up to the last minute. People were packing up around me, loading the truck, and I just managed to get it done. I'd sung my heart out and we said 'That's the one' and went home without even listening to it.'

The venue for the *King Of Fools* recording was Beltwood House, South London. Rumour has it that the Queen Muvva spent her wedding night there. The band were offered it by a group of churches who owned it, and the big rooms with wooden floors were ideal. They were able to record the drums in an old dining room and do some of the vocals in the tiled toilets. For four weeks they stayed there, feeling cold.

The process of recording an album seems to focus the minds of the band on certain subjects. With *King Of Fools* their thoughts turned to commitment, looking for ways of expressing their desire to follow their king. Perhaps this came out of a year when they had gone out on a limb by going full-time, and were unsure of the future.

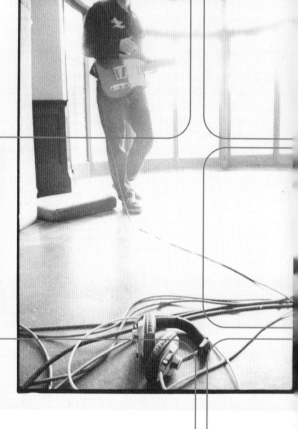

London 05.96 - recording 'White Ribbon Day'

3A
54 TMZ 16 4 KODAK 5054 TMZ 17 5 K

delirious? 67

Stories Behind the Songs

You could say that Martin has come a long way since his day on children's TV. The jumper has gone and the songs have grown up. In certain lights, though, it seems like nothing has changed: the songs that come out of Martin today are still a strange concoction. Alongside a distinct God-focus, he places tunes that breathe on the heart. Near the subjects that many people reject, he places tunes and phrases that they like. For Martin the tension between beliefs and friends, which existed when he was at school, continues to be felt in his songs. Instead of retreating from the world, this time he faces it head on. Through his songs, Martin is determined to join the worlds of God and pop.

If you think about it, it's actually quite ridiculous that Delirious? should sing about their faith so openly. When they pay so much attention to the music itself, why let the side down with lyrics that are only going to put people's backs up? The truth is that getting a reaction is exactly what the band want to do. If it was open arms they wanted from the pop world, they would have whipped their shirts off and started singing songs that went *'Sometimes I feel sad / but you're so sexy / so it's all OK'*. They would have played the game.

But they haven't: instead, Martin and Stu G have become co-writers. They turn out songs that work tightly around selected themes. If you want a top four you could try these out: determination, confusion, frustration and simplicity.

Song 1: Summer Of Love
Written October 1997
Written by Martin
Recorded October 1997
First appeared on 'Deeper EP', November 1997

SUMMER OF LOVE

There is a light that shines upon us
There is a heaven, that's where I'm longing to be
Would you please come talk to me.

There is a darkness that falls upon us
There is a blindness that makes me hunger for you
Will you lead me through?

Summer of love: so full of pain
Summer of love: was God to blame?

There is a song I have been singing
It brings the healing, that's what I'm longing to see
Would you please come fall on me.

You probably know that I love a saviour
His name is Jesus and I am living to be just a
faithful one to thee.

Summer of love: so full of pain
Summer of love: was God to blame?
Summer of love: so full of shame
Summer of love: God knows your name.

'Summer Of Love' is one of those songs that falls into the 'anthem of hope and pain' category. It spends 7.04 minutes brooding its way through an insistent musical hook and a vibe of deep contemplation. If this song were a book it would be one of those complex little ones by a French philosopher.

'I remember,' says Martin, 'at the beginning of the summer of 1997 that we were all pretty tired. We had

The Barn Petworth 03.97 - rehearsals

been working hard for months; releasing the singles and the album as well as doing more gigs than ever before.'

The band were all looking forward to the summer that lay ahead. As well as the usual intinerary, this one had some big festival gigs on the menu, along with a trip to America to discuss their future there. Talking about it in the van, they joked that with so much good stuff packed in, it was bound to be the 'Summer of Love'.

In August, Stew's wife, Sarah, was three months pregnant, but miscarried while on holiday. The trauma affected the whole band and family, causing them to share one another's grief and question why it had happened.

Only a few weeks later, the band and families were gigging together in Jersey when they heard the news of Diana's death in Paris. Like the rest of the world they were shocked and despondent. 'I couldn't believe it,' says Martin, 'another tragedy so soon after the last.'

He knew that he needed to write a song, to find a way of expressing his feelings. As he played around with ideas for lyrics, the phrase they had thrown around with a touch of playground humour seemed to come back to him. Instead of being witty, the phrase was now weighed down with irony: what they thought it would mean was very different to what they got.

Strangely though, as Martin worked on the lyrics, what came out was not only pain, but a belief that the wounds eventually would heal. So, alongside the words pain, darkness, shame and blindness can be found healing, light, hunger and saviour. Did Martin feel these at the time?

'No, it was only months after the song had been written that we could really see the light shining in the darkness. At the time all we knew was that we had to keep going. I think now we know that sometimes positivity has to be a choice; that even though I might not be feeling up, I can still sing about the truth that I believe in. Perhaps I should only write exactly what I'm feeling, but then again there's

often an odd mix of emotions inside: I think at some level you can know joy in the midst of pain.'

The music developed out of a spontaneous melody they had played at a gig two years previously. At that time, Stu G had sung over the tune, and they had both remembered it when it came to writing the song. Musically, the song is unusual in that Martin doesn't sing at all over the outro - the fervent last few minutes of the song.

'I felt this was the first time that I needed to let the music stand up for itself, to give it space to communicate something to the listener.'

Song 2: Sanctify
Written October 1996
Written by Stu G and Martin
Recorded December 1996
First appeared on *King Of Fools*, June 1997

SANCTIFY
Here I am in that old place again
Down on my face again.
Crying out. I want you to hear my plea:
Come down and rescue me.

How long will it take?
How long will I have to wait?

And all I want is all you have,
Come to me, rescue me, fall on me
With your love.
And all you want is all I have,
Come to me, rescue me, fall on me
With your love.

Sanctify: I want to be set apart
Right to the very heart.
Prophesy to the four winds
And breathe life to this very place.

How long will it take?

How long will I have to wait?
And all I want is all you have,
Come to me, rescue me, fall on me
With your love.
And all you want is all I have,
Come to me, rescue me, fall on me
With your love.

Lifted up I've climbed with the strength I have
Right to this mountain top.
Looking out the cloud's getting bigger now,
It's time to get ready now.

The wrenching guitars that fuel the track signalled a new sound for Delirious?. Keeping the sound raw they manage to hold on to the power they had with Cutting Edge tracks like 'I'm Not Ashamed' and 'Mountains'. At the same time, the sound is more current, the lyrics more poetic.

'Sanctify is one of my favourites,' says Stu G. 'At the time it was written it really seemed to capture the way we were feeling.'

To Delirious?, being in the band often feels like a never-ending quest. Although they are often pleased with their achievements, there is always something greater for them to chase after.

'That's a very good thing though' adds Stu G. 'It means we try not to get complacent. In songs you can either tell stories, ask questions or give answers. I'm not sure what this one does. I suppose I see it as simply saying, here I am in that old place again. For me everything comes full-circle in time. Life seems to follow the pattern of 'go out and explore what life's about' and then 'come back and think it all through'. It was at that meditative stage that 'Sanctify' was written. I know that sometimes I try to do things in my own strength, try to make things happen. When I'm down on my face, that's when I've realised that I can't make it on my own. All I want is all God has.'

'Sanctify' started out life in Stu G's head, before he and Martin worked on the lyrics. Like 'Deeper', the song uses

words that don't automatically set the 'Christian psycho' alarms flashing in HMV. The message is strong and clear, but it makes sure that it carries as little baggage with it as possible. There are plenty of words with similar meaning to sanctify (consecrate, purify, make holy), but along with each comes a variety of different associations.

'I'm not satisfied with where we are just playing to a Christian audience,' declares Stu G. 'I really want to prove ourselves as a band in our own right. I suppose it could be confusing to some people. But it's clear in my mind: I want us to be known as a great band. All I want is all He has.'

Song 3: Come Like You Promise
Written in 1994, on the same day that Stu G wrote
  'Absolutely Absolute' and 'Katie'
Written by Stu G
Recorded June 1995
First appeared on Stu G's tape *Have You Heard?*

COME LIKE YOU PROMISE
This is the sound of the secret place
This is the sound that the angel sings
This is the sound of the coming rain
This is the sound of my heart's desire
This is the sound that my spirit sings
This is the sound of the coming rain

Come like you promise

This is the groan from the deepest place
This is the incense that fills the earth
This is the sound of the coming rain
This is the sound of the hope within
This is the song that the prophet sings
This is the sound of the coming rain

Come like you promise

These are the words that creation cries
These are the songs of injustice and pain
This is the sound of the coming rain

Come like you promise

This is another track where Stu G plays it live, looking like he's sawing a stubborn tree stump. It has that kind of 'Achtung Baby' feel - the sound of information, the sound of confusion. Oddly it hasn't made it into the studio for years. Instead, it remains a key striker in the Delirious? away squad.

'I wrote this before I moved down to Littlehampton, when I was playing with a band called String. I wrote it for them, although the song didn't really come into its own until Delirious? got hold of it.'

The song came out of seeing a whole load of situations different people were in. Each of them seemed, to Stu, really desperate.

'Walking down the high street one day, the look on some people's faces seemed to say, "I can't wait for the week to be finished". It seemed like they were living for the next bit of hope, the next temporary solution. It struck me right away that a lot of people are actually surviving rather than living. Later I read in the bible about how all creation groans and waits for it all to be over, for heaven to come. That's what this is about - the sound of the deepest place, the groan that many don't even understand - for something to change.

'The chorus (Come like you promise) is not your typical evangelical Christian way of saying "come Holy Spirit, help us feel good". It's actually saying "Jesus come back and finish all this".'

Song 4: August 30th
Written August1996
Written by Martin and Stu G
Recorded December 1996
First appeared on *King Of Fools*, June 1997

AUGUST 30TH

Thank you for the chance to live again
I will run always for you
Clouds had gathered all around my head
But these hands they lifted me
And I'll tell of this love that saved me.

Thank you for the chance to live again
I will run always for you
Walking closer you are all I have in this life
Only you
And I'll tell of this love that saved me.

And I'll wait for this light to break
I'll come to you, yes I'll run to you
And I'll wait for this light to break
I'll come to you, yes I'll run to you
I'll be one with you.

'August 30th' stands out as an example of the bits of Cutting Edge that Delirious? did bring with them. The vibe is pure intimacy: the lulling repetition of the rhythm and guitars marries the honeyed vocals. These songs broaden the appeal of the band, because as we all know, those young punks may like it loud, but the oldies like to be able to hear the words.

'The song only came to me a year after the accident,' says Martin. 'My brother's wife, Pip, had a serious car crash and, like me, was fortunate to be alive. We both went through the same experience of thinking, once it was over, "Now I'm really going to do something with my life".'

Martin and Pip became close, discussing how they had both reacted to their experiences, swapping stories about how they had dealt with the shock.

'I suddenly realised, through chatting with Pip, that I still hadn't got over it. It made me feel very emotional, realising again that I actually had been saved. I remember exactly where I was: I had put the phone down after talking with her and sat on the bed. Straight away the song came; it just seemed to spill out of me.

'The song is dedicated to Pip, but it was also my way of finally putting the whole experience to bed. I think the tenderness of the song shows just how vulnerable I was feeling at the time.'

Song 5: King Or Cripple
Written September 1996
Written by Martin
Recorded December 1996
First appeared *King Of Fools*, June 1997

KING OR CRIPPLE

King or cripple, what have I become?
Beneath these kingly robes there lies a fragile man
What made me a king can sometimes cripple
All that you give can sometimes rob my innocence

Why do you let us walk upon a cliff so steep
When deep below the sea there lies a bed of gold?
And if this should be our battle place
Don't let us fall, don't let us fall

Keep me, keep me, keep me, keep me

I love to hold the hand of one who held the blind
And saw the leper run into your arms of love
King or cripple they were the same to you
You took a broken man and you treat him like a king

Keep me, keep me, keep me, keep me

If 'August 30th' is one side of the Delirious? sound, and 'Sanctify' is the other, then slap bang in the middle is 'King Or Cripple'. The simple, repetitive, acoustic verse gets chased down the street by a vicious Doberman of a chorus. Manic cymbals and guitars drive the instrumental, revving high. Lyrically it twists through the verses, touching on storytelling, freeform rambling and gutsy preaching. Although it never would have made it as a single, it remains one of the band's best songs yet. Out of all their others, it is one of the most true to themselves.

It was the first song that Martin wrote for the band on a piano, which (according to Martin) 'explains why it only has three chords in it'. The content of Martin's head at the time was a collection of thoughts on the nature of success.

'I just thought, "God you've been so good to me: you've made me successful in a small way." I often struggle with the tension that exists between what people think of me and what I think of myself.

'Some people put me on a pedestal and think that what I do is the answer to everything. But I know that when I get home I'm just trying to work things out like everybody else. At the time I was wondering whether all the things that God has given me had made me a better or a worse person. Had it crippled me?

'In some ways you long for the innocence and naivety of youth, but growing up makes you realise that you can't have it. For us, we grew up when we started to release stuff into the mainstream: we started to get let down. You learn that you can't be an innocent and survive in that scene. Instead, you have to learn the ways to survive. You can become cynical, but every day I fight the tensions inside. I want to be pure and simple, to have a simple faith, yet my life is complex; nothing is simple at all.'

Martin on Songwriting

Songwriting has changed for me. The Cutting Edge stuff was in an era when I wrote it all myself. These days most of the stuff is written by Stu and me. Songwriting's the sort of thing that you're always on the go with, you're always trying to keep open to external influences. My ticker's always going - I have a little book that I write lyrics in. It helps to be in a creative environment, and a band is the best way of getting that. You're constantly pushing each other and trying to keep it all fresh.

Tim on Tone

My tip would be about tone. I'm not the most technically competent player, but I've learnt that it's important to pay real attention to tones. You can play one chord on a Bontempi organ out of a cornflakes packet and it does nothing for people. You can play the same chord on a concert Steinway and it could make someone cry. When you're in a band there's not always room for everyone to get in all the notes that they want to play because you need to keep the space.

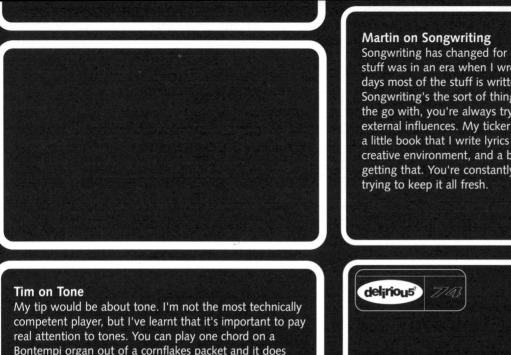

Jon on 'King of Fools'

It's a hypnotic dubby line which I love to play live. As ever, it's a simple but, hopefully, groovy cocktail, with a few cherries on top.

delirious? 75

Stu G on That Solo

An interesting thing is, on 'Promise' it was the first time I'd ever used a Les Paul; we had just got it in for that track. All the sound comes simply from the guitar and a new amp that I'd just bought. I set it to this vintage sound, and laid the track down on the second take, solo and everything. I just sat down and thought of a couple of ideas and then it was there. It was fun.

Stew on 'Mountains'

There's that bit in 'Did You Feel The Mountains Tremble?', just before the pre-chorus when it goes 'And we can see that God you're moving...'. That bit of drumming was inspired by an Elvis Costello track. I just heard it on the radio and loved the poppy sound of the drum without the snare. So I whack the snare off and use it as well as the floor tom and the tambourine.

part 3: *popwork*

Life on the Road

There was once a rumour staggering around that Delirious?, on arrival in Belfast, demanded limos to take them the short distance from the airport to the venue for their evening gig. Furthermore, according to the whispers, they would only be happy if each member was provided with his own limo for the ride. Woe betide the person who failed to ensure the seats were made of the finest pigskin.

The reality of life on the road for Delirious? is sadly less glamorous. Instead of personalised travel requirements and demands that are always met, it's all long drives, scummy dressing rooms, sweat, tears and cheap hotels. After four years, there are plenty of nightmare stories to be told. But alongside them are memories of adrenaline-charged experiences that trigger shivers and grins.

Delirious? are at their best live. Before they first went into the studio they were regularly playing to audiences topping 600. Their following was not built on tricky marketing campaigns or whirlwind promotional tours, nor did they establish themselves by blagging their way through to people's unguarded subconscious. Instead they built up their following over time.

The way it all started was by one invitation for the band to go and play just outside London. It seemed that this particular youth worker was tired of shipping his group down to Littlehampton every month, and thought instead that he might save himself a bit of hassle if he brought the band up to see them. The gig was a success, and before long Tim was opening dozens of letters each week inviting the band to go and play all around the country.

In this way, the band grew in response to the demand for their music. Looking back, they describe their growth as 'organic': becoming stronger over the years. The decision to go full-time was only made on the back of regular requests to go and play.

Having someone else take care of the promotional side of these events had its good and bad points. One advantage was that it meant minimum hassle for the band: all they needed to do was turn up on the day. It helped them form good friendships with fans and promoters alike, who knew that they were contributing to the growth of the band. Today, if you mention doing a gig in a certain area of the UK, Tim will immediately fire off a list of at least ten names of people who could help with promotion in the area.

On the down side, the band forfeited a big slice of control each time they accepted an invitation. Although the gigs always seemed to go well, there was the odd occasion when staying in someone's house after a late gig would strike terror into the boys' hearts.

'I remember Stew and I stayed in someone's house once,' says Jon, 'and the guy's wife had just left him and emigrated to South America. The guy sounded pretty down about it and we both felt really sorry for him. When we got back to the house we stopped feeling sorry and started feeling worried.'

The walls were covered with mould and the floor was home to an insect collection that would have been the envy of any medium-sized zoo. Jon, being the kind of hygienic person who won't even share a glass with someone, spent the whole night sitting on the corner of the bed wearing a hat and itching a lot.

Then there was the time when Jon delivered one of his 'compliments disguised as a criticism'. While being given a lift back to his host's house, he turned his attention to the vintage Fiat that was transporting them. 'This car's so rough it's cool.' he said. The comment didn't get the warmest of receptions, and they continued in silence until they reached her house. Once there, Jon found himself in a room without a door in a house without a dustbin. Again, he didn't get much sleep.

Once the band had started to work with pluggers and mainstream promoters, they were introduced to a whole new work ethic. Some call it 'the blag', and early encounters left them dazed and confused.

Stew remembers one particular gig they had been booked to play at: 'It was a three-day free festival promoted by a Manchester radio station. We had been told by the radio plugger that it was a pretty big deal that could lead on to all sorts of other opportunities.

'We left home at 5am and arrived tired, but excited by the prospect of playing to the 55000 people we had been told to expect.'

What greeted them was not a crowd large enough to fill a stadium, but a rabble small enough to fit into a bus. Less than 60 people had turned up - a figure which made the 100-foot stage, 25 burger vans and 100 portaloos seem a tad excessive.

When the band talk about their music getting inside people's heads, one of the head-invading methods that gets them most excited is the live show. However, after only a few months of three or four gigs per week, they all realised that they could not keep it up forever. The situation may have been different if they had been doing nothing other than gigging, but as it was, the birth of Furious? Records had drawn on all of their talents in such a way that each member was clocking up over 40 hours per week in the office.

In the January of 1997 they decided to spend another six months gigging frantically, after which they would take a break for a while. This was to give them time and space to promote what turned out to be one of their most exciting ventures ever. In the autumn of 1997 they started the d:tour.

Over the course of two weeks the band and their 25-strong crew took to the road and played ten gigs to over 18000 fans. The tour had been in the pipeline for months and had taken considerable planning. The starting point was the idea of reaching a wider audience.

Previously, when the band had played at the request of regional promoters, they had found themselves in venues like churches and sports halls. These places helped to keep costs low, but made sure the band remained an underground act - the chances of music fans turning up at a sports hall one night in the hope of catching a great gig have always been slim.

With the activities of the opening months of '97 it seemed right to the team at Furious? Records that the band got out and started to play venues that were more accessible. Playing in the same places as Blur and The Verve would give the gigs an extra stamp of authenticity that could be vital for people who were strangers to the band and their message.

Another part of the build-up to the tour was the realisation that the band held complete responsibility for the visual side of their appearances. Previously they had been limited to taking with them a few coloured lights. The d:tour, with its big-boy venues and decent budgets, would be something else.

Apart from the band, the key player in developing this side of the show was Andy Hutch. Having met the band in 1996, he had moved to Littlehampton and had taken the unofficial role of official photographer. Andy was a photographer by trade, but had an interest in video. Together with Stew, he worked on ideas for the show.

'We were trying to do two things,' he said. 'Sometimes the video was there to expand on the lyrics of the song - like the people dressed up as fools in 'King Of Fools' - and sometimes it was just an artistic thing, there to look good.'

In each gig the 400-square-foot video screen fired the punters with images of the band, the crowd, playgrounds, limos, businessmen, waterfalls, and anything else that came to mind. The overall effect was stunning: at times amusing and at times inspiring. Although the ticket prices had risen from when the band used to play at one end of a sports hall, all agreed that this was a show well worth the money.

The desire to produce something creative, and not to get stuck in a rut of bland imitation is something that covers all that the band do.

'We've got the creator of the universe on our side,' says Jon, 'so we should have some kind of head start when it comes to being unique.' Instead, for Jon, many of the bands that have come from the Christian scene have been pale imitations of something unique. While it is impossible to break away from your influences, it is important for the band to focus continually on finding fresh ways of expressing the contents of their heads.

The aim of the band is broad. At one level it is to inspire young people within the church to make a difference in whatever they do. At another you would find the desire to make people smile when they go to a gig or hear a CD.

'And,' says Stew, 'our aims go right up to the very pompous idea of wanting to change the way that people view Christianity. I knew nothing of God or church when I was 20. If I can now play a little part in making that change for other people, then I'm happy.

'One of our best chances for doing that is in the live show. Everyone's different: some might start thinking when the music drops down and the show goes quiet; and others might get inspired by the chunky, full-on, grab-you-by-the-scruff-of-the-neck songs like 'Come Like You Promise'. For me, though, it's 'Obsession' that always does it. No other song that we do can let your mind wander at the same time as being really explosive.'

Despite all of these opportunities to get out, play and put the message across, life on the road is a bittersweet pill. They are husbands and fathers first before they are musicians. Although the rapid growth of the band's popularity since 1997 has been an exciting fulfilment of a

dream, there is potentially a cost to bear in mind. The tension between what they feel called to at home and what they feel called to at work can be great, although they work hard at having as much time as possible at home.

'I think,' says Stu G, 'we see more of our families now than we did when we were working for ourselves in the week and gigging at weekends. I know we see more of them than if we were businessmen working in the city. There is a tension there, but our families are as committed to what we do as we are.'

People have suggested to the band that they might consider working flat out for a couple of years and then retiring. To Martin and the rest of the guys the idea doesn't quite hit the mark.

'It's vital that we keep on progressing creatively, even if we don't come out with anything financially. I would rather look back over my life and just think we did some incredible things, pushed the standard up and were an inspiration to people, than end up sitting round a fat swimming pool with a big house. I think God would be pleased too.'

Littlehampton 01.97 - loading the truck

A Day in the Life -
The Filming of the 'Deeper' Video

7.00am
Depart Littlehampton.

9.15am
Arrive at the location: the roof of a five-story office in central London. Start by unloading the truck and getting the gear up onto the roof. This involves squeezing what amounts to a small house into a lift the size of a toilet cubicle. No easy task, but with the help of a few onlookers contributing valuable advice ('No, no, no...you don't want to do that...'), we manage.

9.29am
Amusing incident while loading Tim's Hammond Organ in to the lift. Bloke says 'What's that?' Tim replies 'It's a Hammond Organ.' Bloke says 'Your organ, eh?...ha ha.'

9.37am
Excitement outside the offices below; murmurs from the staff are heard, wondering who the group could be. There is just a slight air of disappointment when they find out who the band are (or aren't, to be precise).

9.39am
Debrief with the crew. Steve, the producer and man in charge, runs through the schedule, quietly displaying the sort of confidence that only comes from experience. He introduces the crew and tells us their jobs and we tell them ours. Actually, he tells us theirs and we look confused - a grip, two runners, production manager, first and second cameramen and a sound man. They try to explain what they do, but time is money and our heads are tired. It all becomes clear later.

10.00am
One of those life-changing experiences: I've always suspected that film crews spend a lot of time wearing puffa jackets and eating bacon sarnies. Now I know it to be true.

10.35am
While the crew are setting everything up, it's wardrobe time for the band. There's a big box from Siesta (The *Only*

Name in British Skatewear) and there's a bit of subtle psychological warfare going on as people rifle through the stuff. ('No, no, Stu, those shorts are great, you don't need the top too...' You know the sort of thing.) 11.15am First take. Steve decides to start off by shooting each individual member of the band standing on what can only be described as a big rotating cake stand. Martin's first up, and after a couple of takes (where his performances are greeted with much shouting and encouragement) his strutting and swaying is easily on a par with Jimmy Nail.

11.30am
Trouble. The particular roof that we are filming on does not belong to the people who said we could use it. Apparently it belongs to their neighbours, who have sent up their security guards. Steve takes them over to one side for 'a quiet word' and that's the last we hear of it.

12.06pm
Cries of 'There's a hare in the gate' mean that everyone has to stop what they are doing and hang around for a bit. I decide to take matters into my own hands and try to rescue the poor animal, but I can't seem to find it.

12.30pm
Jon decides to do his take in a pixie vibe - sitting on top of his amp, smiling strangely as the world spins by. What a pro.

12.38pm
Our Stew seems to be getting a little upset. He's managed to blag himself an armful of free cymbals for the shoot, and has been waiting on the delivery from Windsor since 10am. A quick call reveals that there is a slight problem. 'There's been a slight problem,' explains the person at the courier's office. 'Where are my cymbals?' says the drummer. 'Birmingham.'

12.56pm
It's nearly been three hours since we last ate, so the runners go off in search of another medium-sized supermarket to bring back. While we are eating, we get

chatting to Ken, the grip (the one that pushes the camera about). Ken tells us about working with Oasis, filming naked women, and what he thinks of a couple of the female onlookers. Ken, it would seem, is not a feminist.

1.34pm
It's time for Stu G to take centre stage and be filmed on the spinning cake stand. Knowing that Stu is not exactly what you would call 'shy and retiring', there is great excitement as he gets up, looking like a cross between Bobby Charlton and an eighth century druid. He delivers.

2.03pm
Steve, whom we all trust as he reminds us of John Peel, explains that he wants to film the song with lots of pauses at certain points. Everyone is then to run around, and he will speed up the action to fit the gaps in the song. We spend the next 25 minutes playing a game of bizarre Musical Chairs, without the chairs. Each time the music stops we hop, run, dance or shake as much as we can. People in nearby offices stop and watch us.

2.28pm
Feel sick.

2.31pm
More trouble. It seems that we're making too much noise for the office below, home to *Loaded* magazine. Not wanting to put them off their afternoon rounds of Solitaire, we turn the music down.

2.47pm
The next set of shots are of the group bunched together, and by this time people are feeling a little tired. Martin comments that he understands why pop stars take drugs, what with all the waiting around. However we have no need for drugs as Ken treats us to another round of 'Ken the Grip Speaks his Mind on the Subject of Women'.

3.21pm
Joy! The arrival of the long-lost courier with cymbals. He looks strangely tired and wanders off muttering something about the M40.

3.29pm
Things are set up and we're ready to film. Halfway through the second take, a tennis ball wings its way over the roof, bounces on the camera track and goes back the way it came. People look around in confusion, but nothing else happens, so we carry on.

4.10pm
The shot is 'in the bag' and there's just about time for one more. The boys set up down one end of the roof, and the camera will roam among them. The sky has got a bit cloudy since lunchtime, but a couple of the band (you can work out which ones) are looking a bit red on top.

4.53pm
Midway through a take a pair of scanky trainers and a bog roll come sailing through the air, landing in the middle of the band. *Loaded*, it would seem, have finished their Solitaire competition. We carry on.

5.15pm
More bog roll. This time Rusty the Roadie strategically positions himself within eyesight of the phantom toilet accessory dispenser. It doesn't happen again.

5.56pm
The light is going and Steve calls it a day, happy with all that we've got in the day - 18 minutes of footage. While packing up he comments that the band seem very normal for people that are about to 'make it'. They laugh.

KEN

London 03.97

delirious? 85

AA 1:100

Furious?
Records

Furious? Records

So by now you're pretty well familiar with the way the band work, right? You know that the band favour doing things differently, that given the choice they'd rather try out other ways if it means avoiding being boxed in. Those of you who are partial to a little DIY psychology will have already been wondering why this is so. How can it be that five blokes from an urban dead-end get the idea of running their own record label? And how come, with next to zero experience, they succeed? The answer, it would seem, is to be found in - where else? - childhood. Not the band members' literal childhoods, you understand, but the time when things began for the group. Back when everything was new and unfamiliar.

'It all started about the time of the first tape,' says Tim. 'We had just recorded the tracks for the people at the event: it had never occurred to us to set up a record company. We were producing so few tapes that there was no real need anyway.'

And so there came into being the first ....ious?. This first venture was Curious? Music - a banner under which the material would be published. This was a reaction to a series of conversations Martin, Stew and Tim had had with various people working in the UK Christian music industry. They had been advised that if they wanted to get the songs out to the churches they ought to sign a publishing deal with an established company.

'We had a hunch that the songs would spread themselves,' says Tim. It seemed obvious to not only himself, Martin and Stew, but also to their friends: people got hold of the tapes, worked out the songs and sung them with their friends. Why involve a third party to clutter up a natural process?

So it began. The tapes sold, slowly at first, gathering momentum as the weeks went by. Thinking that it might be a sly way of getting some extra business, Tim had put the phone number for his studio on the tape. After a

couple of months he almost wished he hadn't. 'We got calls all day long: we were constantly having to interrupt sessions to take phone orders.'

As the money started to come in, they opened up a charity building society account (they didn't think they were significant enough to warrant a proper bank account). As they both worked in the studio, it was down to Martin and Tim to handle the orders. Once demand reached the level of 15 orders each week, they handed over to their mother-in-law, Heather Thatcher, who set up a packing office in Sarah's old bedroom.

'It was about this time that we decided to draw some money out of the account and get a new phone line put in,' says Tim. 'The trouble came when people carried on using the old number. People would call the studio asking for tapes and I'd tell them they'd got the wrong number, suggesting they call 01903 733031. I'd wait for them to call that number, answer it, and take their order. Sometimes this worked fine. Sometimes people thought I was a fool.'

'I remember taking phone orders,' says Martin, 'when people would start to ask me if I knew who Martin Smith was and whether he was a good bloke.'

And so we see the beginnings of Delirious? and Furious? Records. They still have the same phone line; they still distribute product themselves; they still treat themselves in the same way.

'At the end of the year,' says Tim, 'we raided the bank account and all went out for a meal.'

'It was our way of saying thank you to ourselves for doing all those gigs for free,' says Stew.

This meal thing still features heavily in the Delirious? subconscious. Many is the time that the Furious?

Barclaycard has picked up the tab for a night out for employees, friends and strangers. Much of this comes from Tim: a shrewd businessman - clearly without him Furious? would be nowhere near what it is today - but generous to the extreme. Halfway through the 'Happy Song' on the second Cutting Edge, tape Mr Jupp butts in with a primal scream of exuberance and energy ('yeeeeeaaaaaah'). This is the same Tim that loves to share his excitement of the good times with those around him; the same Tim that picks up the tab.

But enough of food, let's get back to the action. We left Martin and Tim answering the phone in the studio.

'News spread pretty quickly about the music,' continues Tim, 'and it wasn't long before we were getting calls from Christian bookshops all around the country. They were always confused by the time they got hold of us. Normally what had happened was that a few people would have gone into the shop asking for the tapes. As we'd never sent any sales reps around, the bookshops obviously wouldn't have a clue who they were talking about. So they'd get on the phone to their friends at the big UK Christian labels asking them if they knew where the tapes came from.'

'Because Tim and I had worked on the scene,' continues Martin, 'we knew most of these people at the labels anyway. Soon they realised that there was a demand for the music and they approached us with various offers. Things seemed to be going well as they were, so we carried on.'

This decision prompted the boys to start thinking about selling to the bookshops direct - until then it had mainly been fans that had been phoning up. To present a more professional image, the release of the third Cutting Edge tape coincided with the launch of the label. Furious? was alive.

When 'White Ribbon Day' went into high street record stores in February 1997, many thought that this was a momentous occasion, symbolic of the impact that Delirious? were about to have on mainstream culture. In fact, that symbolic act had taken place years before, when the band's local branch of Our Price had agreed to stock copies of the Cutting Edge tape.

'At first', says Stew, 'the guy in the shop only took one tape, but soon he took five at a time...'

'Because,' continues Martin, 'we were giving it a little plug at the Cutting Edge events - telling people they could go and buy it from there.'

'And every time you went shopping with your wife,' says Tim, 'you would totally by chance find yourselves outside the shop, so you'd pop in and see the tapes on the shelf.'

And so, unintentionally, the band had started doing what they would be desperate to do later on: getting their music out to a wider audience. What they learnt in time was that merely getting it into the shops was not enough; they needed to be able to get it out of the shops too, and that meant securing the vital extra ingredients of airplay and media attention. Ironically, the novelty wore off when they realised that the store was taking an 86 per cent cut of each sale.

As the operation grew, so did the need for space. Ever the entrepreneur, Tim rented and refurbished the two floors above his studio. Before long, Stewart Smith Design moved his computer, printer and mammoth selection of pencils into one end of the large office. At the other end came Jussy McLean: provider of backing vocals, both live and in the studio, for most of the band's first three years. Having given up her job at the local bank, Jussy came on board for two-and-a-half days each week to look after the sales of the tapes and the now increasing number of gigs.

According to Martin, this was a key time for the growth of the label. 'Tim was spending most of his time doing the gigs, and I was doing all the work in the studio. We wanted to keep control of the whole thing, but we didn't know where we were going with it. It seemed important that Tim could give it lots of his time.'

If the band were unsure about exactly how they wanted things to end up, they were pretty clear about how they didn't want things. As each of the boys had experienced the Christian music scene, they had been able to learn from the good and the not so good. It all helped them put together a company that tried to have as much integrity as possible.

As the business ethics began to form, so did the image of the label. Stew was largely responsible for this, even though as a designer he had previously found many of his clients in the corporate sector. The chance to let himself go with something cool was a welcome break from the clean lines and subtle colours of company reports. Unintentionally, he filled the first two Cutting Edge tapes with bold colours - yellow for the first and purple for the second - so that people began to refer to them not by their number, but by their colour. The third tape caught up with the idea and was called *The Red Tape*. Characteristically, they decided not to follow through with a bold green or blue for the fourth tape, instead Stew chose an indescribable blue and called the tape *Fore*.

This sort of behaviour is quite usual at Furious? Records: it is a combination of not wanting to get stale and predictable, and the desire never to take things too seriously.

The recording that directly followed the final Cutting Edge tape was the live CD, 'Live and In The Can'. In December of 1996 the fans were treated to an hour's worth of the boys live. As if that wasn't worth the pennies, both the CD and the tape came in a unique tin can. 'It cost a ridiculous amount of money to package,' says Tim, 'but apart from the odd limited edition, few people had really done it before. I love the fact that it doesn't fit in the CD racks in stores and really stands out.'

For Martin and the rest, 'The money is there to support the creative. The album was pretty cheap to produce, so we had plenty of room for creativity.'

It was in April of 1996 that they sat down with Tim's sister,

Nykki Jupp, and talked with her about taking over from Jussy - who had left to pursue a career in motherhood. Nykki had been doing very nicely as a Legal Executive and was considered to be insane by many of her friends for jacking it all in for a bunch of Christian musos. The band were aware of the risk too: they had gone full-time only weeks before, and agreed to take her on when they weren't even sure whether there was going to be enough money to pay themselves, let alone anyone else. Still, as well as paying their bills on time, Furious? Records have vowed never to let money stand in their way.

Nykki's arrival was timed perfectly: she turned up just as the band were about to drown under a flood of offers to play at various gigs. According to Tim, 'There's always been a strange element to the timing of things with Furious?. We seem always to have got the people we need just in the nick of time. It was like that with Tony, our manager. We had known him for a while, but as we began to understand how important it was for us to be out in the mainstream, we realised that we couldn't manage it on our own. We needed someone with experience to guide us through it.'

In many ways, Tony and Nykki are the backbone of Furious? Records. The band have evolved from being a hands-on force, turning up to their desks at the office each day, to spending the majority of their time out of the office either recording or promoting. And so it is vital that there is an extension of the band, an arm that functions, guides and carries out the business while other parts of the body carry out their own related work.

One thing that the band are kind of proud about is the fact that, apart from on a couple of occasions, they have never asked for gifts. The ethos has extended throughout their work, even to the sales of albums and singles. 'We have never told people to go out and buy our stuff to support us,' says Martin, 'We've just said to people that they should only buy it if they like it.'

The occasions where they have asked for gifts have been pretty special. It was as they decided to go full-time that

they realised the need for some kind of transport.

'Our church,' says Tim 'decided that they wanted to give us something. We had seen this Mercedes van that we thought would be able to carry all of us as well as our gear. We got a picture of it from the dealer and stuck it up on the wall on the day that people had decided to give their money. We ended up with £7000 (not quite enough for the Merc) and got a call the next day from someone who was selling a VW people carrier. It seemed like the right thing to do so we bought it, even though it probably upset all those who thought they were giving towards some luxurious Merc, but instead saw their money represented by an ageing VW. We were still kind of at square one: needing some way of transporting all our gear around. To buy a lorry we needed £10 000 and I knew a lady who had offered to help out once before.'

So one morning, Tim decided to give her a call. She told him that she'd discuss it with her husband. Five minutes later she called back. They'd love to give them the cash, but could Tim be round to collect the cheque within half-an-hour as she had to take the dog to the vets.

It turned out that buying the Merc would have been a mistake as even the lorry became overweight in time. As they used to drive home from gigs in convoy, the band got to know every route home that avoided weighbridges. And who said Christians couldn't be rock 'n' roll?

To finish off this look at the business side of Furious? Records, it might be good to check out one decision they made that everyone thought was stupid. It was in December of 1996 - only eight months after they had gone full time - that they decided to take no further bookings beyond the early part of the following summer. The reason for it was that they wanted to do their own tours, to get out on the road and visit new places and people. They wanted to put on a show that would blow people away - one that would be a million miles away from the days of sports halls, overhead projectors and an underground following. In order to do this, there would have to be at least three months before the tour when the

band wouldn't play, so as to generate a little hunger among the gig-goers.

'At that time we were doing at least 12 gigs each month,' explains Tim, 'and at each gig people were spending on average £2 per head on merchandise. Giving that up was a huge risk to take, even bigger than when we all gave up our jobs.'

However, it all worked out: the autumn of '97 saw the d:tour take the vibes around ten great UK venues. Although they might have been financially better off had they stayed with the regular local gigs, breaking away allowed them to spend more time travelling and recording.

'We don't know how things will work out,' says Tim. 'So far we've grown from employing one person to employing nine. It will probably grow even more in the future and I know that I would be disappointed if we couldn't help other bands get their music heard.'

'Although,' adds Stew, 'it is strange: we started this business so that we could retain control. What happens when you become a record company and start signing people? Have you become that thing you worked so hard at to avoid?'

This sparks a discussion (it has sparked many of them in its time). The truth is that nobody knows what the future holds, just as no one knew what it held when they opened their building society charity account.

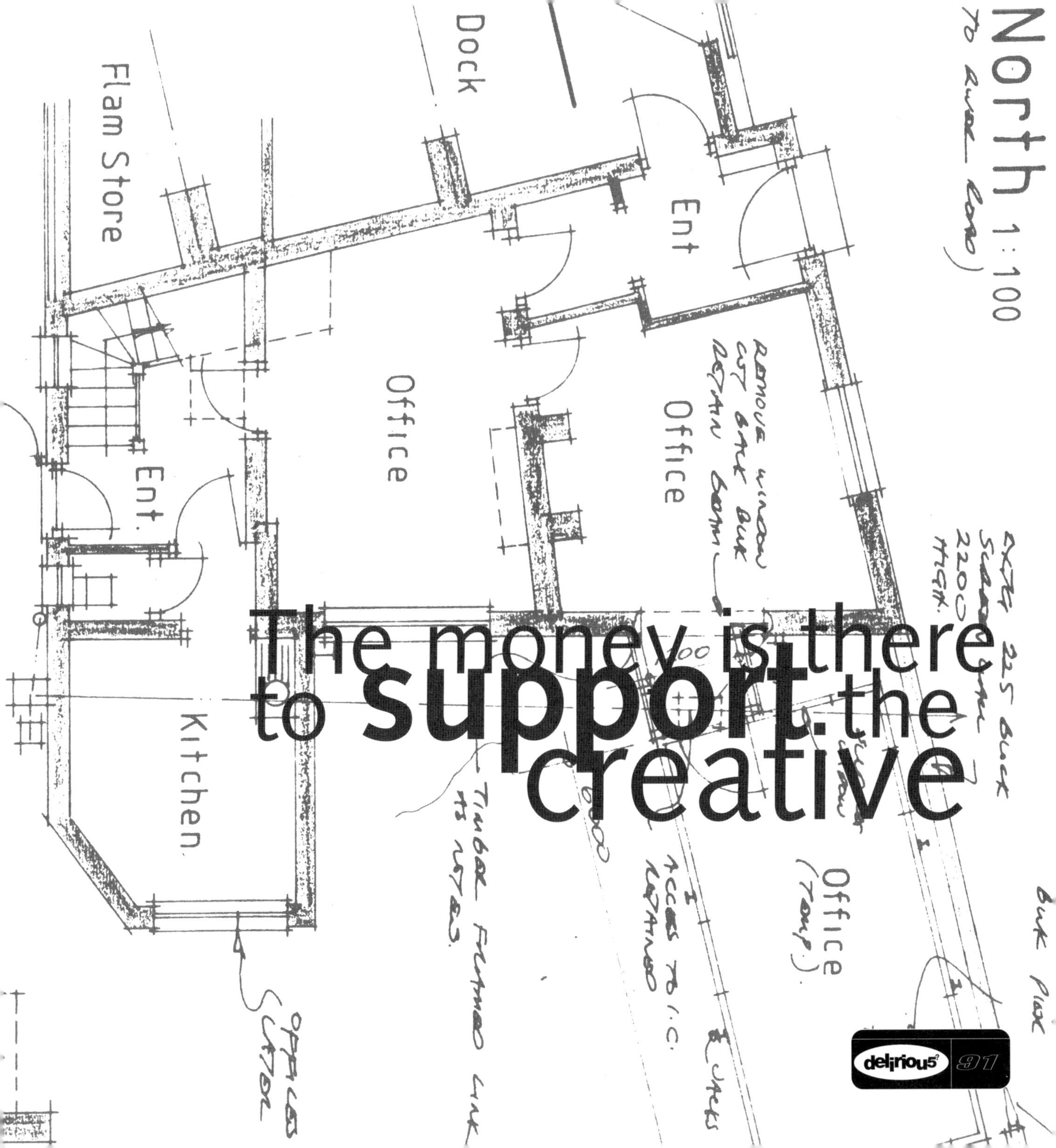

North 1:100
To River Road

Dock

Flam Store

Ent

Office

Office

Ent.

Kitchen.

REMOVE WINDOW
CUT BACK BLK
REMOVE BEAM

EXTG 225 BLOCK
SIDEWALLS
2200 HIGH.

The money is there
to **support** the
creative

TIMBER FRAMED LINK
TO OFFICES.

ACCESS TO I.C.
RETAINED

OPEN LED
SLATTED

Office
(7DEEP.)

BLK PIER

delirious 91

Fame

When Delirious? started to release singles they climbed aboard the train marked Media Promotion, and so began their journey to build a public profile. From multinational corporations to local charities, platinum-selling pop stars to amateur dramatics societies, the media is the mother of all tools for getting yourself known. TV, press, radio and all the rest are without doubt the best way of making sure that your voice is heard by the people. At its best the media can change anything from thoughts to governments, at its worst it can do the same. Plenty of people have used it for good, and even more have used it to bloat their bank balances.

But enough of this preaching, and back to business. On the brink of their assault on the charts, the boys' media education was somewhat lacking. Their seaside home town is the sort where headlines rarely rise above the interest level of 'Man, 74, dies'. The throb and whooosch of London (just 74 miles up the road) is cushioned by miles of genteel countryside that overall makes Littlehampton a thoroughly pleasant place to retire to.

This is not entirely true, for there is one inhabitant of Littlehampton which had a greater influence on the band than just providing them with Almond and Dung Beetle Facial Scrub. The town is home to The Body Shop, the international beauty products chain famed for ethical trading and its stand against testing on animals. In just 20 years, husband and wife, Gordon and Anita Roddick, built an empire so large, with a voice so loud, that visitors to Littlehampton often believe that they are the unfortunate subject of some elaborate practical joke. Motoring down the A259, the sight of the head office's pagoda backed up by stadium-like warehouses, is hard to forget. The business is a lifeline to the local economy, an inspiration to anyone planning on building a public profile.

The band had had some experience of 'fame'. Their on-stage performances meant that people quickly formed impressions of them based on what the spotlight picked out: Stu G looked scary, Martin looked spiritual, Jon looked cute, Tim looked nice and Stew looked cool. But in those early days they didn't want fans; they wanted friends.

Until 1997 they travelled to gigs with someone to mix the sound and someone else to do the lights. There were no roadies and the band would set everything up themselves, and take it down again at the end. This meant that after a quick change out of sweat-heavy t-shirts, the band would be back out the front after each gig. In between packing down bits of kit they would chat with anyone that wanted. Today, the hardcore of early fans still feel like they know Delirious?, and share in the good times as well as the bad. 'When you got to number 20,' wrote one old-timer 'it felt like we were at number 20.'

One of the reasons that Stew does what he does is The Jam. It was the steady beats of Rick Butler that got him into drumming, but his influence went way beyond that.

'When I was really into The Jam,' reminisces Stew, 'they played at the Brighton Centre. Me and my mates stayed outside the venue for the whole day, just waiting to get a chance to see them. In the afternoon they came out and we got their autographs and chatted. From then on they weren't superstars, they were my mates.

'I try to treat people as intelligent human beings. If they want to get an autograph then that's fine by me: I don't think that it's going to severely damage them. At least by chatting to someone you're showing them who you really are. Most of the time people see you through the eyes of a journalist or a cameraman. At least things can be a bit more real when you meet people face to face.'

These post-gig chats and 'can you sign my forehead?' meetings seemed to be a part of the Cutting Edge Band routine. But after a year of being Delirious?, things began to change. Almost overnight, the method of contact with the fans transformed itself from the above-mentioned

forehead signings into a whole strategy that would mean days and days of hard work. From out of the blue came the issue of image - 'Do the band look like they're a band?' was the frequently asked question that bounced around the Furious? Records offices. As if from nowhere, the band had to get used to spending whole days waiting for a three-minute twitch of filming, and then not get paid at the end of it. But most confusing of all was the sudden realisation that it was time for the band to promote themselves.

When people talk about the Delirious? early days, one word that is always guaranteed to come up is 'underground'. Basically, it means that the news about the band spread by itself, from person to person. It was neither directed nor initiated. It just happened. As soon as 'White Ribbon Day' had a release date marked by an orange square on the wall planner, the band knew that they had to get the message out and encourage people to go out and spend their money on them.

'Up until then we had just been gliding along,' says Martin. 'We had been working hard and had made some good decisions, but we hadn't pushed it in anyone's face. All throughout the early days it felt like God had been raising it up. As soon as we got to the singles, we felt the tension. It was the first time that we had ever consciously pushed ourselves on people. We never told people that they had to buy the singles to support our 'ministry', but all the same it felt strange. We wondered how you could do it all and be a Christian. Can you be a spirit-filled Christian and attempt to be a pop star?'

Can you?

'Yes, I think you can. But ask me again in a couple of years.'

The whole concept of image was thrown into the melting pot as well. The band had always been 'into' clothes to a certain extent, always enjoyed following trends and all that. When 'White Ribbon Day' was released, someone suggested that they should try to look more like a band.

They did have a point. At the time, Tim was into shirts and jeans a la Oasis; Martin was into the Cocktail Lounge look (waterfall shirts and oversized suits); Stu G, Stew and Jon had all set up camp firmly in the Skatewear part of town. The discussions bubbled underneath the surface for nearly a year, and in time they all realised that it was less of a crisis and more of a point of debate.

The whole issue got finally put to bed at the beginning of 1998 when Sparrow (the US Christian label that had signed the band in America) sent their Creative Director over to get a whole suitcase full of photos for their marketing teams. Like chicks after their mother hen, Delirious? followed her around as she took them shopping. What came back were five young men that looked like they had finally found out what a mirror was for. At last they wore colours that suited them.

But you may be thinking, 'Whoa! How did we get here? Just a few paragraphs back you were banging on about how they were struggling with the tension of having to promote themselves, and now this? Frantic shopping that makes Ivana Trump look like a penny-counting OAP.'

Good point. Anyone have any thoughts?

Stew has: 'It is something that we do all feel slightly uncomfortable about, but let's be honest, it is great fun wearing nice clothes. There is a danger when you get to a certain level as a band, and you can't do everything yourself. You have to get other people in to help carry the load, and often it turns out that they're very good at load carrying. That's what has happened in America. Furious? Records cannot distribute our stuff over there; it's physically impossible. So we hooked up with Sparrow and let them handle it. They're a great label and they like to do things the best they can.

'If you're going to have photos taken, you might as well make sure they look good. We want to have photos that are good enough for *Q* and *Rolling Stone* magazines, as well as for the smaller Christian publications.

'I hate calling it a job, but promotions are vital to what we do. We can't play every week to everyone in the world, so we have to find other ways of communicating with people: the media is how we can do it. 'Rather than avoid the music business altogether because of a few bad areas, we want to get involved and kick some purity back in.'

Make no mistake, it's not all nice clothes and photo shoots. Take TV, for example. According to Martin, 'TV is a complete exercise in boredom. You often have to get there at six am for a dress rehearsal at seven. Then you have to wait for hours until it's time for your bit to be filmed.'

The band try to relax in the aeons of down-time they go through.

'We try and spend time chatting to the other people there,' says Martin. 'A lot of people say we're the first people that have ever asked about their kids or about themselves. We don't lay our beliefs on people heavily.'

Fame is a funny word to use with Delirious?. They do get recognised from time to time, although that doesn't always go as smoothly as you might expect. Imagine the embarrassment of settling down at Number One Court on a June afternoon to soak up the Wimbledon vibes, when someone comes up to you and says, 'Is it you? Is it really, really you?'. You reply that you are most definitely you, but then the person sitting next to you develops an interest and joins in, 'Who are you then?'. It's all enough to give you an identity crisis of gibbering proportions.

What the band try to do is not to believe the hype. A limo is a limo, but in America it doesn't signify the band's importance, it signifies the fact that a limo is cheaper to hire than the three taxi cabs you would need to transport the whole team around.

In the same way, having security guards present at an in-store signing is not an indication of the manic hysteria the band's presence could induce. They are there because the store doesn't like getting stuff nicked.

The final thoughts on the subject are from Jon. Having always been into the underdogs, liking the bands that no-one else likes, he finds himself getting a bit worried about what might happen if they really did get big.

'It scares me so much that I always seem to be saying to my mates and my family, "if you ever see me stepping out of line, you have to tell me."

'I was reading a book by Douglas Coupland (author of *Generation X*) and something he wrote reminded me exactly of something I had just been thinking about. It was about the dangers of chasing after tomorrow, of not being content with the here and now. The man's got such a good take on this generation: he understands how it can either end now or we can do something about it. He puts a lot of hope in his writing.'

And so do the band. If they get it their own way, they will have a world platform for their music. That could mean fame and fortune - and an even greater effort to keep their feet on the ground.

Stu G looked scary, Martin looked spiritual, Jon looked cute, Tim looked nice and Stew looked cool

America - The Great Unknown

Popular opinion would have it that the Pilgrim Fathers had it a lot worse than the Pilgrim Great Great Great Great Grandsons. OK, so way back then New York was little more than a slab of mud. So what if they had to start from scratch after a life-threatening sea voyage? They got to wear black and were all a dab hand with a chisel and a bit of 2 x 4. What faced Delirious? on their first voyage across the sea was for more challenging. Instead of fuelling up in the land of plenty, the boys found themselves in the middle of a nightmare that would reduce even the most capable person to a total wreck.

In February 1996, Stu G went to California to do a recording session with a young man named Jeff Searles. The easy-going Californian introduced Stu G to more of his easy-going Californian friends, and pretty soon our Stu was himself feeling pretty easy-going, in a Californian kind of way. One such friend he met was a man by the name of Dushan Bilbija, who was involved in various bits of youth work at his church. Dushan was buzzing about a youth conference they had held nine months previously. Over five hundred people had turned up, many meeting Jesus for the first time. The plans were all in place for a repeat conference to kick off that summer, but alas, they had no worship band to help out. He asked Stu G if the band would consider playing, and as soon as Stu got back and put it to the rest of the guys, he told Dushan they would be delighted to take part in the event.

As the conference approached, Stu G received various e-mails from young Dushan informing him of the progress of the event, and of the nature of the arrangements. It seemed that, because well over 500 people were expected, the organisers could afford to put the band up in a hotel complete with swimming pool.

A week before they were due to leave, the excitement about their first-ever foreign trip was at fever pitch. This was also the time for another e-mail from LA, saying that the numbers were just a little lower than expected and would they mind if they ditched the idea of a pool in favour of staying in a house that would be empty while they were there. Slightly disappointed, but ready to soldier on through this great difficulty, Stu G replied on behalf of the band: of course they understood.

Another e-mail arrived. Dushan's easy-going Californian implant seemed to be malfunctioning: only 25 people had booked into the event. It was too late to cancel, so the band duly boarded the plane and headed for LA.

When they arrived after their 11-hour flight, they were on a high. This was really it: rock 'n' roll. Paul Burton (soundman and lifelong 'Dukes of Hazard' fan) simply couldn't contain himself and marched off to ask members of the LAPD if they knew the way to Hazard County.

Dushan turned up with his friend Matt Smith, and delivered the news that their van was outside the airport, but had broken down. It would take just a short while for them to go and hire a replacement.

Patiently, the band whiled away the three hours that it took Dushan and Matt to find a van. When they returned, the band were told that, in the interest of killing two birds with one stone, they could immediately do a little sight-seeing and pick up some more sound equipment for the conference. Having come from a town where PA companies didn't tend to base themselves in the more architecturally noteworthy quarters, the Littlehampton five-piece were understandably intrigued. But only briefly.

Once they had completed their chores, they finally started their four-and-a-half-hour drive up the coast to San Louis Obispo. To keep them amused, Matt and Dushan treated them to action-replays of some of the longer scenes of 'Friends' episodes and excerpts from 'Dumb and Dumber'.

On the way they stopped off to get some food in Santa Barbara (by which time it was 9pm local time, 8am British Summer Time). At any other time Santa Barbara would have been a delight, a slightly eccentric but elegant home for the rich and laid-back. For the travellers who hadn't slept in 36 hours, the pelicans that populated the bay all proved too much. Paul fell asleep at the table and the others stared about them in a cocktail state of paranoia and extreme confusion.

They pressed on after their meal, and arrived at their destination before midnight. They met the pastor - who wasn't too happy, considering he had just spent thousands of pounds getting them over to play - and were taken to the house where they would all be staying.

There were two bedrooms downstairs with makeshift beds, and a luxury room upstairs with bathroom and jacuzzi en suite. They all agreed for some reason that Tim deserved it the most, and the crew all quickly retired.

Within minutes of getting into his king-size bed, Tim was aware of someone else in the room. He opened his eyes and saw a man who introduced himself as Bill, the owner of the house. He reached beneath Tim's bed, pulled out a camper bed and settled himself down on the floor next to the keyboardist. Then he started whistling. To cap it all, they were joined by his dog, who spent the rest of the night trying to decide whether it was Tim's or his master's head that he found the most comfortable.

The next day was the start of the conference. As predicted the numbers were low, and any last-minute flood of bookings was yet to appear. The attendance was still at 25. At least they could get to know one another.

There were actually 26 people at the conference: an A&R man from Integrity Music - another major player in the US Christian music market - had flown over especially to catch the band he had begun to hear about. Luckily, he and the rest of the audience could get nice and close to hear Martin sing, as the only PA installed consisted of one microphone and a single speaker, neither of which worked.

The conference went well enough, and after the three days it was over. The next gig was to be back down in Anaheim, a wealthy suburb of LA, where the band were to play to over 1000 people. That day, Dushan and Matt had arranged for the band to pick up some PA equipment in preparation for their first major gig in the States. They arrived at the depot ready to pick up a U-Haul trailer to help transport their gear down the coast to Anaheim. Unfortunately, the office had shut at 12, half an hour earlier. After a volley of frantic phone calls, they discovered that their U-Haul had been delivered to the conference address they had left an hour before.

When they finally arrived at the venue for their evening gig, they were surprised to hear that their performance start time had been moved from 8pm to 6pm. As it was then 5.40pm, they performed the quickest set-up ever, and were ready to start 35 minutes later. As they struck their opening chord at 6.15pm, the surge of power blew the fuses and sent the auditorium into semi-darkness and the band into a blur of echoey drums and not much else.

They carried on, and it turned out to be one of their better gigs: all candle-light and passionate singing. On the way out they were paid ($500) and Dushan, a little embarrassed after the U-Haul incident, told them of a real treat he had in store for them. Along with a few others, they went to Fat Bob's Blobby Steak House and enjoyed some big food. Unfortunately, their American hosts had forgotten to bring any money and it was left to the Brits to stand the cheque.

The next day they spent on Venice beach, sunbathing and having a good time. Then it was back up the coast for a couple of gigs at San Louis Obispo and Redlands. Because they thought that the conference was going to have over 500 people in attendance, they had brought with them a fairly large quantity of merchandise. It didn't seem right to take it back with them, so they found a local Christian bookshop and sold them the lot at an enormous discount.

There was one final adventure to be had before returning to England. Matt Smith had been telling them about how

great skydiving was and had offered to take them himself. Being a bit keen, he even had a special crash-helmet with a video camera on top that he promised to film them with while they were plummeting towards the earth in tandem with an instructor.

They arrived at the airfield in the middle of the desert. Paul and Stu G were to go first, and dutifully put on their little jump suits. They all then settled down to watch a training video that spent most of the time focusing on the dangers of skydiving, briefly mentioned how to jump out of the plane, but seemed to ignore the whole process of landing. The nervous Brits brought this up with the instructor who brushed their concerns aside with a nonchalant, 'Don't worry about landing. I'll teach you about that once we're on the way down.'

They were then asked to sign a lengthy contract which Tim told them meant they were agreeing that if they died, they wouldn't sue. Not knowing whether to be scared or amused, they carried on.

Before Paul and Stu G could jump, the staff had to try to get the plane working. At first the radio wasn't working, and then the battery went flat. On the way to the runway the pilot remembered to check the fuel, and realised they didn't have enough. Having filled up, the plane refused to start again. Eventually a set of jump-leads was produced and the plane was started, as if it was an ageing Ford Escort in Battersea.

Finally, Paul and Stu G jumped, one after the other. From the ground the others watched as their friends fell straight down for 45 seconds. Matt Smith appeared to be showing off a little, spiralling around in the air. They later found out that his chute had got tangled up and his emergency technique of opening his second chute was not working either. Right at the last minute, his chute untangled and he landed safely. It was, he told them later, the closest he had ever come to death.

High winds prevented the rest of the band from trying to kill themselves, and no one was that upset. No one, that

is, apart from Jon, who has always had a sweet tooth for danger.

There is one final story to add on. Two weeks after they returned home, they got a call from the bookshop that had bought all their unwanted stock. They had completely sold out and wanted to know if they could get any more.

It was this trip, the California Nightmare, that started things off for Delirious? in America. Without it, their nerves may have been a little more intact, but the word would have taken a lot longer to get out.

Since the summer of 1996 the band have made numerous trips to America. For each of them it continues to hold a certain magic: the type that can only exist when you've thought about a place for years and years.

'America,' says Stu G, 'plays a big part in my life. I've been fascinated by it since I was a kid: the mix of cultures and the size of the place.'

Like all young boys growing up in England, Jon thought of America as being the coolest at whatever it did: TV, sport and fast food.

But for the band which those little boys would later form, America is much more than a large playground. The size of it makes potential rewards seem huge, and since their first trip over, there have always been a handful of companies begging the boys to sign their chunky powerpop vibes to their particular label.

It took a long time before they were ready to sign with Sparrow. The deal had to be right: it had to include the possibility of mainstream releases as well as those into the Christian market.

'I think in many ways the American Christian music market is very similar to the UK's, it's just a whole lot bigger,' says Jon. 'In the same way that we could perhaps have decided to stay within the Christian scene over here, we could have an option to do that over there. But we need to be trying

to get our music out to the people that need to hear it most. We need those mainstream releases over here and we need to keep that in mind when we're in America too.'

Delirious? want a world platform for their music. They want to get their message right out there. On the way, they have to deal with America' with its huge Christian music industry and powerful religious undercurrents. The five lads have a big job on their hands - there are plenty of those who have done far better in the UK but have failed in America - but they approach it with their usual determination.

'When we decided to go full-time and have our own record label everyone said we would never do it,' says Tim. 'When we put out our first single, no one in the industry believed we would try again. When we started talking about doing the same thing in America, people told us we'd never manage to do well in both the mainstream and the Christian markets. All we know is that we've got to go with our hunch, with what we believe we're here for.'

Eventually a set of jump-leads was produced and the plane was started, as if it was an ageing Ford Escort in Battersea.

To cap it all, they were joined by his dog, who spent the rest of the night trying to decide whether it was Tim's or his master's head that he found the most comfortable

Niagra Falls 10.97 - wet and wild

Creation West. Washington State. 08.98

delirious? 101

TONY PATOTO:

Facts of life: After being born in Montreal, the Patoto family moved around a fair bit (Mr P Snr worked in the printing industry) and ended up in England when Tony was 14. Having been a 'reasonable reprobate' at school and college, he failed as many exams as possible before getting involved in films. He was a production runner on that eighties classic, 'The Hand of Death', which then led on to work on other projects (commercials, corporate promos and the like). That was then followed by a stint as a sales rep for Fender Guitars, but the white collar life didn't suit. Tony started touring with bands as either a tour manager or a guitar technician, the last one being with Voice Of The Beehive. 'It was terrible,' he says. 'Far too much drugs and rock 'n' roll for my liking.' He then leapfrogged from one record company (Power Records) to another (The Total Record Company). He stayed at Total for seven years, working with the likes of Space, Sash, Aswad, Right Said Fred and Mr Blobby. Tony met Delirious? through his friend Andy Piercy - he who produced the early part of the Delirious?/Cutting Edge catalogue - and told him how he was getting tired of all the dance music that surrounded him. 'I was saying how I wanted to find a good guitar group who were playing eight minute epics like Led Zeppelin used to.' Andy had just finished recording the first Cutting Edge tape and introduced Tony to Martin. Over the years they talked together regularly as Tony gave them advice. Life got more intense for the band when they decided that they wanted to release 'White Ribbon Day' as a single. It was to Tony that they turned, and through The Total Record Company that they distributed their material.

Delirious? highlight: 'Seeing 'Deeper' get to number 20 and seeing the d:tour '97 take off: both of those were things that we had planned for a long time, and when they happened it was amazing. It's been great to see the American thing take off and get the chance to meet people that have been my heroes: meeting Steven Curtis Chapman was a particular highlight. From a gig point of view, a highlight would probably be Brixton Academy or Greenbelt '98.'

View from the band: 'The man who comes to work with smile, a loud laugh and a wise word.' - Jon
'Always, always, always up for a laugh. This Canadian manages to implement the things that others can only dream of achieving. Great guy with a big heart!' - Stew
'Knowing and working with Tony is like living through an atomic explosion every day. Every morning he tells of sleepless nights when he's figured out how to change the world, and then if we don't like the idea he would have thought of ten other solutions by lunchtime. Tony does not think London, LA or Lisborn, he thinks Universe, and I'm so happy he walked into mine.' - Martin
'Tony always brightens up my day; he laughs at my jokes something which always scores highly in my book.' - Stu

name: Tony Patoto
age: 34
born: Montreal, Canada
home: Guildford
favourite meal: Caesar salad with grilled chicken
favourite d:song: 'Lord You Have My Heart'
relationship to band: Manager

Caribbean 09.95 Terri & Tony

Canada 05.97 Tony: the ideal travelling companion

Furious? Records 11.98

ANDY HUTCH:

Facts of life: Once he was born, Andy and family moved to Aberdeen where they stayed for a long time. When he was not at school, Andy worked in a theatre as a stagehand and lighting assistant. He wanted to be a cameraman, a photographer or a lighting director, but eventually ended up studying Photography at Napier College, Edinburgh. Having gained his degree, he worked for an advertising studio in Newcastle, after which he landed 'the best job in Manchester' as assistant to one of the best-known photographers in the city. After three years it seemed like time for a change, and Andy moved to Lancaster to work for a charity which offered photographic services to other charities. This gave Andy the chance to get stuck into editorial photography, as well as plenty of travel. One of his clients was producing a magazine that Stew was designing, and the two of them met. 'I knew that Stew and I would get along when I sent him some shots of a band. Most of them were pretty standard, but I had also included a couple which I'd dropped on the darkroom floor. Stew said those ones were his favourites.' This was the beginning of it all: Andy came down to shoot the guys in the very first week that they had gone full-time. Just before he left, Stew told him that if he was ever thinking of moving down to the South they would be keen to use him for all sorts of work. 'And that's precisely what has happened: I moved down a year later and have been involved in all sorts of ways.'

Delirious? highlight?: 'The first night of the d:tour, in Folkestone. As the intro sequence started I felt an intense buzz in the air, as if it was the start of much more than just a gig. Another highlight was when we played Brixton Academy and everyone watched the video to 'August 30th'. The kick for me was that it was such a simple idea, but it engaged people completely. I remember being stood next to Blur's lighting director when they played at Brixton a few months before. It all looked so good and what he was doing seemed so complex that I thought I could never manage it myself. That's the way it's been for us: you look ahead and envisage these extreme scenarios, like playing to 40000 people or packing out major venues that your heroes have played. When you get there, it often seems totally natural and right. Every time we've been in this situation I've always been pleased, but I've also been looking forward to the next thing.'

View from the band: 'Next door neighbour, friend, cook, lighting man, photographer and fellow Beetle bum. What greater compliment can I give?' - Jon
'Never before has there been so much creativity and visual awareness wrapped up in so shrewd a businessman.' - Stew

name: Andy Hutch
age: 31
born: St Andrews, Fife, Scotland
home: Littlehampton
favourite meal: gnocchi
favourite d:song: 'Absolutely Absolute' and 'Heaven'
relationship to band: Live Art Director and Photographer

Hutch
'To use light you have to be a light. He's a lightbulb of bright ideas. Thanks for the smoke and mirrors.'
Martin
'In the relatively short time I've known him, he's become a great friend. We like the same sort of stuff so we see a lot of each other outside work. I couldn't imagine being on the road without him.' - Stu G

PAUL BURTON:

Facts of life: Grew up in Milton Keynes and left school to take up an electronics apprenticeship. At church he met a bloke called Adrian Thompson and started being the guitar technician for his band called Split Level. One night, at a gig at the Breedan Bar in Birmingham, the house engineer was so hammered that they had to send him home. Adrian knew that Paul had done a little bit of mixing at church and he asked him to do the gig. Within a year he was doing their sound as they played the mainstage at Greenbelt Festival. Paul was made redundant and so wrote to a company called ICC for a job as a studio engineer. They already had a studio engineer, but they did need an electronics vacancy filled, so Paul signed up.
That was how he and Martin met - Martin was the studio engineer. After a couple of months Martin left and so Paul took on his job. The Cutting Edge events started and he got involved after the first one. Eventually, totally overworked, Paul decided to leave ICC, move to Littlehampton and set up Ground Zero, a sound and production company. He borrowed a little cash and bought the PA that was used for all the CE events. One year, later a friend - Matt Jones - moved down and became a partner.
When the band decided to go full-time, he could have joined in, but it didn't feel like there was enough work. These days it works out well: about 15 per cent of Paul's work is for the band ('and they're my number one priority'), and the rest of his time is with other acts.

Delirious? highlights: 'There were two gigs that were better than the rest: one was at the Roxy in Hollywood. It was in July '98 and the band were playing well in front of a crowd packed with industry people. They were really clear about their faith and I was proud of them. The other great gig for me was at Greenbelt in '97. What they did was so different for the festival that it caught people's attention. That one was very worshippy.'

View from the band: 'He's the sixth member of the band.' - Stu G
'At the end of the gig Paul will say exactly what he thinks. Sometimes he's hard, I always trust him.' - Martin
'Paul's the only person on the road that understands my insanity. We're tuned in to the same white noise.' - Jon

name: Paul Burton
age: 27
born: Bedford
home: Littlehampton
favourite meal: steak
favourite d:song: 'one of the new ones'
relationship to band: Front of House Sound Engineer

Chronology

October 1992:	The Cutting Edge event is born, with Tim, Stew and Martin forming the core of the band.
October 1993:	*Cutting Edge One* is recorded. It goes on sale 2 weeks later and soon sells out.
February 1994:	Stu G and family move down from Kettering to the Littlehampton. Stu becomes the official guitarist.
May 1994:	*Cutting Edge Two* is recorded and released. Again, early sales are swift.
July 1994:	First ever 'Cutting Edge on the Beach' open air gig takes place, attracting 1000 people.
October 1994:	Cutting Edge Three (*The Red Tape*) is released and Furious? Records gets underway, distributing product throughout the UK Christian scene.
June 1995:	Having played a few gigs, Jon now finalises the line-up by becoming the permanent bassist.
August 1995:	Martin, Anna and Jon involved in car crash.
October 1995:	*Cutting Edge Fore* recorded.
December 1995:	Each of the five members decide to pursue the band full time. They rename themselves Delirious?, as it rhymes nicely with Furious? and Curious? (the name through which Martin & Stu G publish their songs).
March 1996:	'White Ribbon Day' is played in public for the first time.
April 1996:	The band go full time.
May 1996:	Nykki Jupp joins Furious? as Office Manager.
July 1996:	The band travel to America for the first time.
December 1996:	*Live and in the Can* released.
February 1997:	'White Ribbon Day' released in the UK. It reaches number 41 in the singles chart.
May 1997:	'Deeper' released. It enters the chart at number 20.
June 1997:	*King Of Fools* released. The first Delirious? album charts at number 14.
June 1997:	Delirious? play the Champion Of The World event at Wembley Stadium.
July 1997:	The fourth and final Cutting Edge on the beach pulls in over 8000 people. The third single, 'Promise' is released the next day, charting at number 20.
July 1997:	The band travel to America to discuss a possible deal with Sparrow/Virgin.
October 1997:	The d:tour visits ten venues throughout the UK. In the middle 'deEPer' is re-released. It goes in at 36.
March 1998:	A double album of the Cutting Edge tapes is released in America.
May 1998:	*King Of Fools* released in America.
July 1998:	Among other gigs throughout the summer, the band play to 50,000 people at the Creation festival.
Summer 1998:	*Cutting Edge* and *King Of Fools* go global, reaching, among others, Australia, New Zealand, South Africa, Holland and Hong Kong.
November 1998:	*Mezzamorphis*, the second album is completed. Plans are made for the release in 1999.